The Nurture Method

The real-life guide to raising your business and family

By Heather Roberts

The Nurture Method:
The real-life guide to raising your business and family

ISBN Paperback: 979-8-89576-181-6
ISBN Hardback: 979-8-89576-182-3

Published by:

We did it! Thank you Josh for being willing to take that first step with me. Emmy, Ben, and Kate y'all are living proof we can figure it out even when it looks messy. I love you all to the tips of my toes. —H/Momma

Table of Contents

Introduction: The Accidental Entrepreneur 7

Section 1: The Startup Phase: When Your Business Is Your Baby 13

Chapter 1: How My Three Businesses Actually Started (And What That Means for Yours) 15

Chapter 2: Your Why, Your Power, and the Courage to Begin Anyway . 22

Chapter 3: The "Oh Crap" System 30

Chapter 4: Money Truths: Cash Flow, Pricing, and the Mistakes We All Make 37

Chapter 5: The Right First Hire (Spoiler: It's Still Not Your Friend) 43

Chapter 6: Taming the Chaos: Time, Energy, and the Truth About Busy 51

Chapter 7: Time Boundaries for Founders (Because No One Else Will Set Them For You) 57

Chapter 8: Why Good Advice Can Still Lead to Bad Decisions 64

Section 2: The School Age Phase: Business Puberty (And Other Awkward Growth Stages) 73

Chapter 9: Prune for Growth and Dial-In with Data 75

Chapter 10: From "That's Crazy" to "That's Possible": The Mindset for What Comes Next 81

Chapter 11: Five Point Guards Don't Win Championships 88

Chapter 12: Know Your Numbers (Even if Math Makes You Twitchy) ... 95

Chapter 13: From Solo to Leader: The Awkward Truth 102

Chapter 14: Milestones, not Mayhem: Planning that Actually Works . 110

Chapter 15: Work-Life Integration (because Balance is Bullshit) 116

Chapter 16: Avoiding the Bright-and-Shiny When Your Business Gets Boring 123

Section 3: The Teenage & Empty Nester Phases: Raising a Business that Runs Without You.. **131**

Chapter 17: Is Your Business Scalable? (A Hard Look) 132

Chapter 18: Thinking Like a CEO: The Shift that Changes Everything ...139

Chapter 19: The Black Friday That Broke My Systems..........................145

Chapter 20: Culture over Credentials: Scaling Smart 152

Chapter 21: Why You're Overwhelmed (and What to Do About It That Actually Works) 158

Chapter 22: Keeping Your Cup Full..166

Chapter 23: The Village You Need (And Why You Can't Do This Alone)...174

Chapter 24: Your Business Is Grown—Now What?..............................181

Conclusion: The Life Cycle of a Business 189

A Note Before You Go 191

The Accidental Entrepreneur

You know that feeling you get when the universe throws you a massive curveball, and you're standing there wondering, "What the hell just happened?"

Yeah, that was me in March 2007, when a wrong number—on a landline, no less—accidentally kicked off the multi-million dollar consulting business that would change our whole damn lives.

Before I go into that, though, let me back up for a moment to explain how this came about. My husband Josh and I were just babies when we started dating, only 19 and 20, and we got married a couple of years later. We made a deal early on: whoever got the better job offer, that's where we'd go. I was a nanny. Josh was in sales. So, guess whose career we followed? We spent the next 14 years criss-crossing the country. Our first stop as a married couple was Louisville, Kentucky. After a quick nine months, we headed to Springfield, Missouri, then six months later to Maryland. We'd just settled in there when I learned I was pregnant, and we were off again, to New Jersey, this time not long after our first child was born. We kept relocating every couple of years as Josh climbed the corporate ladder, living in Kansas City, Memphis, and St. Louis.

By 2007, Josh had been promoted to VP of Sales. We also had three kids under 12—all born in different states—and were tired of packing up and moving at the drop of a hat. We were exhausted by the constant moving and ready to put down roots. But as long as Josh stayed in corporate, that wasn't happening.

I was in full-time stay-at-home mom mode: chauffeur, chef, event planner, conflict negotiator, and unpaid executive assistant to four other humans and a dog. We had the idea to "do something on our own," but we had no clue what it would be, or how to even begin. In the meantime, we moved back to my home state of North Carolina, bought a house, and got the kids settled in school. I really thought Josh would continue to work, and I'd stay in my role of managing our domestic chaos, that my day-to-day life would basically stay the same, just in a different location.

Spoiler alert: everything changed. I literally laugh out loud now at how unbelievably naive I was. I had no clue what was coming (and it is the best thing that could have happened!). The day that changed everything started out normal, until Josh walked into the kitchen with a funny look on his face. He'd just finished a call with a guy from Canada who owned a furniture company and was hoping to sell his products on Walmart.com. To this day, I have no idea how he got our number, but I thank the stars he did. The thing was, Josh had just spent the last two years developing an e-commerce sales channel for a major ready-to-assemble furniture company. In other words, the help this guy needed was exactly in my husband's wheelhouse of expertise. Instead of simply saying "wrong number" and hanging up, he'd ended up in a 30-minute conversation about e-commerce strategy.

We knew we had something. We'd landed our first client before we even picked a name for the company—the demand was real. But to be honest, we were like fish out of water. Josh had the corporate background, and I had a plethora of organization, scheduling, and problem-solving skills from my time as Mom in Chief, along with knowledge of things like customer service and finance from being a volunteer. But neither of us had ever built a business from scratch. There were a million questions: Who's doing what? What do we charge? And where the hell do we find more clients, because what are the odds that another one would just call out of the blue?

Starting a business changed everything—our budget, our relationship, our sense of stability. We had to completely rewire how we thought about money, work, and marriage.

And of course, once people heard we were starting a business, the well-meaning advice started rolling in. But no one had actually done what we were trying to do. Looking back, I wish we'd been clearer from the start about what kind of help we actually wanted. But learning to set boundaries as a founder? Bahahahaha! That's a skill set all its own, and one we were just beginning to understand. We screwed up. A lot! Figuring out our roles, our pricing, and where we were going to find clients. It felt like a constant chemistry experiment. Some things worked, and others flopped big time, but we didn't quit. We learned, adjusted, and just kept showing up.

I wish I could say this started by creating a detailed scope of work for our first client, actually determined how many hours we'd spend on their tasks each week—including prep time—and set an hourly rate intentionally on the high side, knowing that many potential clients would want to negotiate. But I can't. We didn't do any of that for the first year or so. We were just so excited to be making some money. Crazy, I know, but as an entrepreneur, I'm sure you can relate.

It took about 18 months before I really started looking at the time we were putting into a client vs the amount we were being paid. I learned that we needed to build in some wiggle room because some prospective clients tried to negotiate us below our minimum. Once we'd nailed down our pricing, we were ready to grow our client base. I wish I could tell you we found a secret formula, but the truth is, for the first few years, this came down to the hustle and grind. Remember, this was 2007, when people were still getting used to the idea of buying furniture and home goods online. For perspective, Wayfair was still called CSN Stores, and its co-founder, Niraj Shah, was hustling just like we were, running around trade shows trying to convince suppliers that e-commerce was their best way to grow. I know this because we went to every home decor and furniture trade show in the United States that we could. This kind of ground-level, face-to-face networking was exhausting, but we were able to build relationships with internet retailers like Walmart, Overstock, One Kings Lane, Rue La La, and the aforementioned Wayfair, who were as eager to grow their e-commerce offerings as we were to grow our client base.

Even with all this hustle, it took time to create a consistent cash flow. Compared to what Josh had made as VP of Sales, our income was essentially cut in half. We had to make some huge adjustments. Annual vacations were put on hold; purchases were limited to necessities, like buying new clothes when the kids outgrew them, when in the past we might have bought something just because they liked it. We didn't have expendable income, period. Everything we made either went to supporting our family or was poured back into the business to help it grow.

I felt guilty about this at the time. I was afraid our kids would feel deprived or miss out because of the tighter budget. The funny thing is, now that our kids are grown, I've learned those fears were unwarranted. They remember trips to the library, going to the town square to hear the free concerts, and playing hide-and-seek in the neighborhood at night. If there's one lesson for parents that I can pass along, it's that kids don't need much to feel rich as long as they feel seen, safe, and loved.

One of the hardest parts early on? Figuring out who did what. I was 100% intimidated. I didn't have corporate experience. I hadn't managed big teams. Josh had the title, the suits, and the resume. But once we started growing, I discovered my years of volunteering had given me the exact skill set I needed to start and run a business. Maybe I hadn't led a team of sales reps or conducted strategy sessions, but I had coordinated teams of volunteers, helped to plan and run events, and kept the budget balanced as president of the PTA. My experience as the family momager meant I brought a similar array of useful skills to the table as Josh had developed in his corporate career.

We figured out pretty quickly that we each had our own Zone of Genius. Josh is a closer. He knows how to get client buy-in, build trust with clients and customers, learn as much as he can about each business and customer, and how to make everyone successful. I'm a systems girl. I love operations, accountability, and marketing. Once we figured out how to stay in our own lane, the business started to take off.

A lot of the same characteristics that make Josh and me good life partners also make us good business partners. We like and respect each other as people, and share a core set of values and morals. We learned early on that adding "co-founders" to our relationship was a whole new ball game. We needed new ground rules. Communication was paramount, but we also needed to make sure we weren't only talking about the business all the time. One rule we set was not to talk about work before 8 a.m. or after 7 p.m., leaving space in our days for us to talk to each other as parents, or as husband and wife. If I had a nickel for each time one of us would pop off with a new idea or solution to a problem...let's just say we wouldn't have needed RSG Sales! We also worked hard to make sure our work selves and home selves didn't bleed into each other, keeping personal disagreements out of the business and not letting our workplace roles transfer into our personal time. For Josh, it was a challenge for him to let go of some control and not micromanage me and my schedule. For my part, I sometimes struggled not to take things out on Josh at work if he'd done something (or not done something) that ticked me off at home. It wasn't perfect by far, but we did the work. And that's what made it work.

On the first anniversary of our business, I gave Josh a little plaque that he still has in his office today. On it is a quote from Martin Luther King, Jr.: "Faith is taking the first step even when you don't see the whole staircase." I think that sums up entrepreneurship. Starting a business means first trusting in yourself to take that first step, even when you don't know where it's going to lead you. Since that fateful wrong-number call in 2007, I have now owned three businesses. RSG Sales is thriving. My pillow business, E By Design, I grew for six years, then sold for a seven-figure exit. The last, Sercy, was a beautiful mess and shut down within a year. All three started the same way: with one shaky, uncertain step.

The Startup Phase: When Your Business Is Your Baby

I've raised three children and built three businesses. As someone who's done both, I can tell you they have a lot of overlap. Hard work. Too little sleep. Constant attention.

Just like kids go through developmental stages from newborn to adult, businesses have growth stages. Each comes with its own challenges and common mistakes, even for experienced entrepreneurs. That's the idea behind the Nurture Method. When you understand what stage your business is in, it's easier to figure out what steps to take next and which advice actually applies to you. Strategies that work for a multi-million-dollar corporation don't apply to a two-month-old e-commerce business. It's like getting potty training advice when your kid is a teenager. Not helpful right now.

The startup phase roughly translates to the infancy and toddler stages. If you're a parent, you remember those years of constant supervision. An early-stage business is the same. It's highly dependent on you because you haven't built the systems or teams that would let it run without you. You're in the "kitchen sink" experimentation phase—trying everything to figure out your identity, target customers, and long-term operations. The business is testing boundaries, building basic skills, and learning to stand and walk. You might have a vision, but it mostly exists in your head. The business hasn't developed its own identity separate from you yet.

Every business is different, with its own needs and challenges. But there are commonalities across startups. Even experienced entrepreneurs make the same mistakes in this stage: keeping systems in their heads instead of documenting them, chasing shiny object syndrome, and hiring based on loyalty instead of skills. The chapters in this section will help you avoid some of these pitfalls and give you strategies for creating systems, managing finances, and hiring the right people at the right times.

Your baby business can't function without you yet. But by the next stage, you'll have more breathing room and separation. You'll get your time and mental energy back. The insights in this section will help you get there.

CHAPTER 1

How My Three Businesses Actually Started (And What That Means for Yours)

Here's the truth: I didn't follow any of the "start a business the right way" advice. I didn't weigh pros and cons or hunt for the perfect niche. I didn't conduct market research or write a business plan. I had a gut instinct, a decent idea, and enough courage (or recklessness) to go all in.

For two of my three businesses, that was enough. And as Meatloaf said, "Two Outta Three Ain't Bad." But with Sercy, skipping the validation step? That mistake cost me.

This book is about what I learned building those businesses—and raising a family—at the same time.

It's about the systems I didn't know I needed until I broke down without them.

The boundaries I had to create once I realized no one was going to hand me the time or energy I craved.

And the choices I had to make when I finally stopped trying to be liked and started trying to build something that could last.

If you're in the thick of it—juggling work, ambition, family, and identity— I wrote this for you.

Because the world doesn't teach women like us how to lead without losing ourselves.

So I made my own method.

It's not perfect.

But it works.

Let me show you how.

Let me step back for a second to give you some context on exactly how each of my businesses came about. I already explained in the introduction how RSG Sales started, which was through the blind luck of an unexpected phone call at exactly the right time. Josh and I do deserve some credit; we may not have generated the business idea out of thin air, but we did spot the opportunity in the wrong-number-caller's questions. Still, I'm not sure that we would have ever landed on that idea if the phone call had never happened. We had the skills to fill a void in the market, but we didn't realize that niche existed until an outside force opened our eyes to it.

E by Design and Sercy both grew out of my time at RSG. In the early days, I wasn't just helping clients with sales; I was diving into their product development too.

One of my mentors called me out: "Why are you giving all this away? Build something of your own."

That comment stuck.

I played with this idea in the back of my brain while I kept working with our clients. While helping One Kings Lane develop a pillow line, I had this moment: I *loved* the work. I could do this every day.

Suddenly, I heard my mentor's voice in my head asking, "So why don't you?"

And E by Design was born.

Sercy's origin was from the trade show trenches. I kept seeing tons of cool little vendors at these trade shows selling all kinds of unique gift items. Remember, this was when Shopify was still in its infancy and social media hadn't yet become a go-to for e-commerce sellers. Etsy existed, but was still just for makers. I thought a niche site that could bring small sellers together would be hugely successful—and it probably could've been, except I built it backwards. (We'll get into those mistakes later.)

* * *

Each of these business ideas came from a different spark. RSG Sales was prompted by someone else's need; E by Design came from me rethinking how I could monetize my skills; and Sercy arose from me seeing an unmet need in the market.

If you're trying to figure out what kind of business to start, those are three solid places to look:

- What do people already come to you for?

- What problems do you keep bumping into that make you think, "Why hasn't someone fixed this yet?"

Sometimes the business idea is hiding in plain sight; you just haven't given yourself permission to pursue it.

Starting a business is a lot like starting a family.

Sometimes it's planned. You do the prep, get the timing right, and feel ready (as ready as anyone ever feels). Other times? It just… happens. You're in it before you even realize it, figuring things out along the way.

E by Design was the "planned kid." RSG Sales? Happy accident. But both worked.

Because the secret isn't in how you start. It's how you show up, grow up, and stick with it when things get hard.

Here's the tricky part about giving or taking business advice: every entrepreneur is different. What worked for me might not work for you. What failed for me might be your big win. That's why I'm not here to hand out one-size-fits-all steps.

The goal is to get you thinking. To give you enough perspectives that you find your own footing. Even if someone else's advice isn't *quite* your fit, it might lead you to the idea that is.

With that in mind, I asked some of my entrepreneur friends how they came up with their business ideas. Just like their industries and personalities, their paths to getting started couldn't be more different. And that's exactly the point.

I hope their stories show you there isn't just one "right" way to start a business—there's *your* way.

Meet Brittany Pickrem of Branding by Brittany, an expert in branding and graphic design services. She's been working with organizations and thought leaders for 18 years. Her passion is using her talents to support those who are doing good things. But Brittany didn't start with a mission. She started with a need. At 17, she was out on her own. That pressure forced her to look hard at her talents and ask: What can I do right now to earn a living?

She figured it out. And she's still doing it on her terms.

Brittany is also a serial entrepreneur and has started two other businesses on the side of her branding work. Similar to my story, one stuck, and the other didn't. In the late 2010s, she dabbled in a personal styling business. This felt like a natural evolution: after all, personal style *is* a kind of branding. Her concept? Help people show up with confidence by styling themselves with intention.

She put it best: "I might be scared shitless, but I'm going to look hot."

But here's what Brittany didn't expect: not everyone sees clothing the same way. Some of her clients had deeper body image baggage, and she realized quickly that this wasn't just about styling outfits. Brittany wasn't willing or able to essentially become a wardrobe therapist. That ultimately led to her closing the business, though she learned a valuable lesson in the process: "It taught me something about how everybody looks at things very differently."

Her latest venture? A line of eco-friendly, chemical-free laundry detergent. This idea came from her own difficulties with sensitive skin and finding a laundry detergent that wouldn't irritate it. She wanted to develop a product to "put goodness into the world," like the clients she works with as a branding expert. So now, she's quietly building this company. One step at a time. No flashy launch. No viral campaigns. Just steady, intentional growth—right alongside her branding work.

Jim Cocks knew pretty early on that the corporate world wasn't for him. But figuring out what *was* took a few tries. He tested out an art store. A supplement brand. A life coaching gig. All before landing on the thing that actually stuck: Level Up, his business coaching business. And the funny thing is, he never set out to be one. "I honestly believe your ideal client finds you," he says. "I never set out to become a marketing or business coach. It wasn't even in my field of vision. But people kept coming to me after seeing my success. That's when I knew I was onto something. The demand was already there."

Danielle Ratliff took a more direct route. After finishing massage school, she bought an existing practice, Serenity Now Massage Therapy, from an owner who was ready to move on.

It was a smart blend of two strategies: lean into what you're already good at, and take over something that's already working.

And it thrived—until it didn't.

COVID wiped out the massage industry almost overnight. But even before the shutdown, Danielle was hitting a wall. The long hours. The stress of running a brick-and-mortar. It was burning her out. She didn't know what was next, but she knew she couldn't keep doing *that*.

So what *was* next?

Turns out, Danielle had quietly built a whole other skill set running Serenity Now. She just didn't realize it was marketable yet.

She'd done all her own marketing. Built her website. Learned social media strategy by necessity. And figured out what she *didn't* want: managing a team, clocking into a location, or sacrificing her schedule. She needed flexibility, remote work, and space to breathe. A creative marketing business ticked every box. But she didn't come to that idea on her own.

"It dawned on me because one of my past massage clients, who worked in graphic design, asked me to help her with proofing projects," Danielle explains. "It all boils down to people for me. I wouldn't have thought to do this until that old massage client reached out to me."

A desire for a more balanced life was also the driving force for Palak Shah. She spent 17 years in corporate America, leading global teams and managing multi-million dollar budgets. She excelled in her role, but learned another lesson, too: "I learned what happens when you build success by someone else's definition and lose yourself in the process."

The turning point for Palak was when she became a mom. "I found myself leaving the house by 7 a.m. and returning just in time to put my kids to bed," she says. "I remember thinking, 'This can't be what success is supposed to feel like.' I didn't want to choose between building a legacy and being present for the life I was living right now. So I started looking for another way."

Palak started first by building a real estate portfolio to build wealth without sacrificing her time and freedom. It was when other women started seeking her advice on making a similar pivot that Palak realized she had a viable business on her hands. "When I saw the pattern in what they were asking—how to build wealth without burning out, how to invest without losing sleep—I knew there was real demand," she says. She launched Open Spaces Coaching to share her insights into building self-sustaining wealth.

Väre Effect founder Jade Green also started her career working for others. She spent 13 years in the trenches of the recruitment industry. During that time, Jade says, "I sat across from thousands of candidates— smart, capable, and often completely crushed. Not because they weren't good at their jobs, but because they were stuck under shit bosses and toxic cultures. That's when I knew: culture was the real problem. I didn't want to just fill roles, I wanted to be the world's largest enabler of humans who are happy at work." This realization led Jade to start a consulting business where she could help businesses fix problems with their culture, leadership, and team dynamics that were the real root of their talent acquisition issues.

Here's another theme you might've noticed: the founders who hit the ground running didn't just follow their gut; they had proof.

Danielle knew she could market because she'd done it for herself. Jim and Palak had people begging them for advice before they even had an offer. Jade saw the need firsthand while she was still a recruiter.

That pattern held true in my own story, too. RSG Sales? We didn't chase it. It chased us. That random call? It *was* proof of concept. Same thing with E by Design. I knew there was demand because I was helping other brands meet it.

So what makes a good business idea? It's not just what sounds good. It's what's *validated*—by experience, by data, by real conversations. If I could give every new entrepreneur one piece of advice, it's this: Before you throw your savings, your nights, and your sanity into a business—make sure it's viable.

Find a mentor who will tell you the truth, not what you want to hear. Do the research. Sketch the plan. And for the love of your bank account, don't skip the validation step like I did with Sercy. That little detour cost me $150,000. Before you fall in love with your idea, get clear on the numbers. If it's a product, know your costs and margins. If it's a service, know your market, your pricing, and what makes you different.

Test it. Talk to real people. Build a waitlist. Sell before you build if you can.

Whatever path you take—don't wing it. *Prove* it.

Because learning the hard way is expensive. I've got the receipts to prove it.

Key Takeaways:

- **Your biz idea doesn't need to be revolutionary**: Opportunities are hiding in problems you can solve, skills you can monetize, or gaps you see in the market. Keep your eyes open.

- **There's no one "right" way to start**: Whether you bootstrap, find a co-founder, or take over an existing business, there's more than one path to success.

- **Don't be a lone wolf**: Learn from others who've been there, but adapt their advice to fit your unique situation. Entrepreneurship is a team sport.

CHAPTER 2

Your Why, Your Power, and the Courage to Begin Anyway

Y'all, if you've survived the toddler "why" phase, you deserve a medal. It hits like a freight train somewhere around age two and doesn't let up.

Why is the sky blue? Why do we need naps? Why can't I wear my Halloween costume to Target? (Because apparently that's not socially acceptable, kiddo.)

Exhausting as hell? Absolutely. But here's the thing—they're onto something.

That relentless curiosity, asking why over and over, is exactly the mindset you need to bring to your business. Because clarity of purpose isn't a nice-to-have; it's a survival tool.

Before you get too far into the what or how of your business, you've got to get clear on the why. Not the cute social media version, but the one that will still matter on the days you want to quit.

There's no one right answer. But you need a real one.

* * *

Your "why" might be practical. It was for Josh and me. We wanted stability and control over where we worked. Palak Shah's driving "why" was similar. She wanted freedom and flexibility to be there for her kids, and building a real estate portfolio was the best way she saw to do that. This didn't turn into a coaching business right away. That passion was something she discovered along the way, once she saw how her approach to building wealth could help others. Your "why" might evolve in the same way as your business grows.

My friend Robert Patin? His why came from pure frustration. He'd been grinding in public accounting for years, making other people rich while barely getting by himself. After yet another dispute with his employers over compensation, his husband looked at him and said, "When are you going to get tired of making everyone else rich and not yourself?" That was the kick in the ass he needed.

Then there are people like my friend Pia Silva, who were basically born entrepreneurs. She knew from day one she wanted to be her own boss. "I've always enjoyed learning things at my own pace, and felt like my brain and my abilities have gone faster than whoever I'm around, and so the idea of working for other people just never appealed to me," she says. Some people just have that entrepreneurial fire from the start.

Here's something no mentor can do for you: figure out your why. Only you know what actually drives you and what you're trying to achieve. And if you don't know yet? Stop everything and figure it out NOW. Don't invest another minute, another dollar, or another ounce of energy until you're clear on this.

While you're at it, also think about what you bring to the table as an entrepreneur. What skills and experience do you have that will enable you to make the business successful? Don't limit this list to things you've used in past jobs. A lot of my greatest strengths as a business leader I didn't learn in a workplace. I learned them by being a mom and a volunteer. If you're a great communicator, planner, organizer, or wrangler of people when you're with your family or helping your community, those are also things you can do as a business leader. Take full stock of your skills, interests, and passions. These are all resources you'll have to draw on, and knowing about them from the start helps you accurately assess where you're strong and where you have gaps you'll need to fill in.

Understanding your skills and goals also helps you to do something else: to realize you don't need to seek permission from anyone else to start your own business. We're all trained to seek permission from the time we're kids, and most of us keep doing it well after we're grown.

Let me ask you something. How many times this week did you take a picture of an outfit and text your friend, "Does this work?" Or write an email and then immediately ask your partner to read it before hitting send?

We all do this shit. And entrepreneurs? We're the worst offenders.

I get it. It feels safer when someone else says, "Yes, that's a good idea." We want confirmation that we're not completely delusional. Plus, if everything goes to hell, at least we can say, "Well, Sarah thought it was a good idea too." But here's the problem with that safety net...

When you're first starting a business, it can be helpful to run the idea by other people. That's the whole "proof of concept" I talked about in the last chapter. But there's a difference between "Do other people want this?" and "Am I allowed to do this?" The first one is about identifying your market; the second comes from a place of fear and insecurity. This might seem like a subtle distinction, but it can make a big difference. If you constantly seek outside approval, it can lead you to water down your vision to please others or delay your action to the point you miss out on opportunities. The bottom line is, while it's hard to have confidence in your own judgment when you're starting something new, you don't want to give away your power to people who aren't living your dream. This is another place where it can be helpful to have that "why" firmly in mind. You're starting your business for a reason. You're the only one who has this vision, you're the one taking the most risks, and, sometimes, even when everyone else thinks you're wrong, the best thing you can do for your business is stick to your guns and what *you* think is best.

Let me tell you about the time my team thought I'd lost my damn mind. E by Design was known for unique, artsy throw pillows. But I wanted to launch what I called "Everyday Basics" (basically solids and stripes). You know, the boring stuff.

My design team looked at me like I'd suggested we start selling pet rocks. "You can get solid pillows anywhere," they said. "This isn't what we're about. This is beneath us."

But my gut was screaming that this was exactly what our customers needed.

So instead of seeking permission and leading by committee, I launched the line anyway. Guess what happened? For the next 18 straight months, a plain navy blue pillow was our number one bestseller. Our. Top. Seller.

If I'd listened to my team and waited for their blessing, we would've missed out on our biggest revenue driver. Sometimes you have to trust your gut over everyone else's opinions.

Does this mean you should completely ignore what other people think? Absolutely not! But it's important to stop and figure out why you're getting outside input and whose validation you're really looking for. Before you seek someone else's approval, ask yourself: Do I actually need input on this—or am I just afraid of making this decision on my own? Over time, you'll start to recognize the triggers that make you want outside validation. Often, it's because you're afraid of rejection or failure, or because the situation is big and scary, things like entering unfamiliar territory, spending a lot of money, making a high-stakes decision, or tackling a new challenge.

Something else to remember: if you feel trepidation about starting a business, you're in good company. Most entrepreneurs do. My friend Brittany from Branding by Brittany knew she wanted to be her own boss, but she was terrified she wasn't "enough." Not smart enough, not professional enough, didn't dress the part. Sound familiar? "I think there's elitism that goes with entrepreneurship," she says. "I thought of an entrepreneur kind of like a stock image. You're in a suit and buttoned up," but that wasn't her. So, for a long time, she took the safe route and worked for other people. Eventually, though, she took the leap. In her first year, she landed a big contract with a client who fully aligned with her mission, and that gave her the confidence to keep following her passion. Looking back now, she says, "I think we can be our own worst enemies by disqualifying ourselves, even when you're perfectly qualified."

My friend Jim Cocks coaches entrepreneurs through this exact fear. The best advice he ever got? "Say yes and work it out later."

He explains, "So many people hesitate because they're afraid of failure, of being unprepared, of the unknown. But most of the biggest wins in my life came because I said yes before I felt ready." He also cautions against waiting until everything is perfect to start. As he says, "Too many people let perfectionism paralyze them. They think their 80% isn't enough. But your 80% is someone else's 150%. The bar you set for yourself is always higher than what anyone else expects of you. So just move. Make the post. Launch the thing. Adjust later."

 Can we talk about money fears for a second? Because they're real, and they're paralyzing. Robert, who's an accountant (so you know he's not exactly a risk-taker when it comes to finances), was terrified about cash flow. He and his husband bootstrapped the business, so they had a lot to lose if things went wrong. It turned out Robert had no reason to be nervous, though. Within 18 months, he'd broken $1 million in revenue.

Palak Shah's biggest fear was making a financial mistake that would risk her family's security. She'd left a safe, 6-figure corporate job to start her own business and was terrified that she would fail in front of everyone. What she learned, though, is that "fear is a byproduct of unfamiliarity, not inability. I pushed through by anchoring myself to a bigger why. I wasn't chasing freedom just for me. I was breaking generational patterns for my children. That made the risk worth it." Palak also discovered another gem of wisdom in the process: "I learned that courage doesn't mean you have no fear. It means you act anyway, because what's on the other side is bigger than what's in your way."

When Pia Silva started her consulting business, she and her husband were living on cash with about $3,000 in their bank account and little available credit. "The big fear was that we wouldn't make enough money to live," she says, but she didn't just work through her fear—she used it to drive her forward. "I pushed through by just hustling harder. That fear made sure that I was at every possible networking event, that I pounded the pavement every day for a very long time to ensure that something was always coming in." Sometimes fear is exactly the motivation you need to get shit done.

But here's where I need to pump the brakes on the hustle narrative, because that mindset can become its own kind of prison. One of the lessons that Palak Shah learned the hard way was that success doesn't require suffering. As she says, "For a long time, I equated hard work with worthiness. If it felt easy, I questioned it. I thought I had to earn my success through exhaustion. But the truth is, ease is often a sign of alignment, not laziness. And when I finally gave myself permission to build from my strengths—to follow what energized me instead of what drained me—everything unlocked. If I'd learned that earlier, I would've stopped forcing strategies that didn't fit. I would've built my business around my fire, not my fear. And I would've scaled a lot faster, with a lot more joy." Read that again. Ease doesn't mean you're doing it wrong. It might mean you're finally doing it right.

Robert Patin had a similar misconception. He, like many people drawn to entrepreneurship, had a workaholic mentality, and the idea that everything had to be a grind aligned with that mindset. He started off thinking he was going to sacrifice all of himself for the business, "which wasn't the reality and doesn't need to be." Starting and growing a business does sometimes mean long hours and hard work, but it doesn't need to mean sleeping four hours a night and never having free time again.

So how do you grow a business without letting it consume your entire existence? Part of it is systems (we'll dive into that next chapter), but a lot of it comes down to how you think about goals.

If you're only setting those big, scary, keep-you-up-at-night goals, you're setting yourself up for permanent hustle mode. And you'll miss all the good stuff: the learning, the small wins, the actual joy of building something.

Don't get me wrong, I'm not saying goals are bad. You absolutely need them. But the way most of us approach goals? That's what's messing us up. Large, 5-year-plan type goals aren't the only option. The better route is to break these down into smaller milestones that give you a path to follow instead of just a destination.

Look, I'm not just making this up. There's actual research backing this. One concept that applies is the "progress principle", which basically says small wins keep you motivated way better than waiting for the big kahuna. Researchers found that making progress in meaningful work is the single most important thing for staying motivated day-to-day. Makes sense, right?

There's also something called the Goal Gradient Effect, which is a fancy name for something we all know is true: the closer you get to finishing something, the harder you work to get there. It's why you suddenly get a second wind when you're almost at the end of a workout, or why you hustle harder in the last quarter of the year to hit your revenue goals.

Bottom line? You're way more likely to stick with something when you can see you're actually getting somewhere.

So how do you break down a terrifying goal into manageable pieces? This is where your why comes in handy again. You need to know where you're going and why it matters. Once you have that clear picture, you can work backwards and identify the natural stepping stones.

Think of it like planning a road trip. You know your destination, so you can map out the stops along the way.

Revenue goals are the easiest example. Before you hit a million dollars (because yes, you can), you'll celebrate your first sale, your first $1,000, your first $10K, and so on. Each milestone gets you closer and gives you proof that the big goal isn't just a fantasy.

The same thing works for intangible goals. Want to be known as the go-to expert in your field? The first milestone might be publishing your first article. Then, speaking at your first event. Then, launching your first course. Each step builds on the last.

Here's the thing: this isn't an exact science. You're looking for that Goldilocks zone where milestones feel challenging but not impossible. Too easy and you'll get bored. Too hard and you'll want to quit.

Timing is tricky, too, especially when you're starting out. You don't know yet how long things actually take, or how often other people will mess up your timeline. (Spoiler alert: it happens a lot.) Give yourself grace while you figure out what realistic looks like for you.

The good news? This gets easier with practice. Once you start setting and hitting milestones, you'll develop a better sense for what works.

Pro tip that'll save your sanity: write everything down. And I mean EVERYTHING. Document each milestone you set, whether you hit it, what worked, what didn't, and what you learned. Your future self will thank you when you're setting next quarter's goals and can actually remember what the hell happened last time.

This becomes your personal playbook for realistic timelines and milestone sizes. Plus, looking back at that list of accomplished milestones is like therapy for imposter syndrome. You'll see proof of how far you've come, especially on days when everything feels impossible.

And for the love of all that's holy, celebrate your wins! Every milestone deserves recognition, even if it's just a happy dance in your kitchen while your kids think you've lost your mind. You've earned it.

Key Takeaways:

- **Get crystal clear on your "why"**: Your reason for starting this business is what'll keep you going when shit gets real. Dig deep and find it.

- **Take stock of your superpowers**: What skills, experience, and resources are you bringing to the table? Knowing your strengths is key.

- **Set milestones, not just far-off goals**: Break down your big dreams into bite-sized chunks. Celebrate the small wins along the way.

- **Feel the fear, do it anyway**: Action is the antidote to anxiety. You don't need to be 100% ready to take the leap.

CHAPTER 3

The "Oh Crap" System

Let me start with something that might seem obvious but apparently isn't: your employees can't read your mind. I know, I know, "Well, duh, Heather." But here's what'll blow your mind: most of us business owners (myself included) completely miss the should-be-obvious implication. If you want your team to know something, it can't just live in your head. Period

And if you're thinking, "Well, I'm solo, so this doesn't apply to me"—hold up. Your memory is not the steel trap you think it is, especially when you're stressed or juggling eighteen different things. Translation: busy parent entrepreneurs who are managing businesses while keeping tiny humans alive are literally the LAST people who should be trusting their brain to remember important shit.

Look, I'm not judging here. I'm speaking from painful experience. In the early days of running RSG Sales, one of the most unfortunately common phrases I heard from Josh was, "Let me guess. It's in your head?"

It became such a running joke that I'm cringing just admitting this. Often, the situation would go something like this: I'd be confidently working on a promotional calendar for Wayfair, not even realizing I'd left Josh and our team completely in the dark about crucial details until someone would ask, "What percentage did the client authorize for the summer sale?"

"Oh, it's 15%," I'd reply casually, like it was completely normal for this vital information to exist only in my mind. Client details weren't the only things I'd do this with, either. I ran our budget the same way for years (much as it pains me to admit it now). I "knew" exactly how much we needed to make in sales each month to cover our costs plus payroll. There were no spreadsheets or formal tracking system of any kind, just me and my mental math.

Was I usually right? Yeah. Was it sustainable? Hell no. And here's what I learned the hard way: even when you don't completely screw things up, this approach is quietly sabotaging everything. You think you're being efficient, but you're actually creating a business that can't function without you being the human hard drive for everything important.

Y'all, I turned myself into the world's most expensive bottleneck. Since everything had to go through me, most tasks couldn't be fully delegated. If I were busy when Josh or another team member needed to make a decision, they'd either have to interrupt or wait for me to finish. In other words, somebody's workflow and focus were going to be disrupted. This also meant I couldn't truly take days off. Even if I was sick or on vacation, I had to keep one eye on my messages in case an employee needed information stored only in my mental filing cabinet. Then came the challenge of training. New hires couldn't peer inside my head to learn from my memories. Growth requires transferable knowledge, and that means first putting that knowledge in a tangible, shareable format.

Running things by memory is also exhausting. Tracking and recalling information requires mental energy, and that can be a big drain on your internal battery when you're trying to run an entire business out of your head. The constant mental juggling and fear of forgetting key information are extra stressors on top of the overwhelming responsibility that comes with being the only one safeguarding key knowledge about the business. Decision fatigue is also much more likely when you're literally the only one empowered to make decisions.

The lightbulb moment came when I finally—FINALLY—created actual budgeting systems. Holy cow! Our profit margins jumped because we could see exactly where money was hemorrhaging. Once expenses were documented, they had to justify their existence. No more "well, we've always paid for that" spending that made zero sense when you actually looked at the numbers.

When it came to critical information like inventory levels, shipping requirements, and discount percentages, keeping it only in my head wasn't just inefficient; it was actually hurting our ability to serve our clients effectively. Realizing this drove me to create a client intake form to capture essential details about their products and pricing structures. With this in place, suddenly, anyone on the team could create a promotional calendar without needing to consult me first.

This is the magic of systems. When you have defined processes for accomplishing tasks and specific places where important information is stored and tracked, it streamlines every aspect of the business. Team members are empowered to complete their work independently. As the owner, it frees up your mental energy for things that will actually move the needle, and spares you the need to start from scratch every time you tackle a task you do over and over.

Now, I can hear you wondering: If systems are so great, why doesn't every entrepreneur have them from the start? I think many people fall into the trap of assuming that systems need to be complicated or require buying expensive, confusing software. As Level Up founder Jim Cocks says, "People overcomplicate systems because they think it'll help them look legit. But your business doesn't need to look 'established,' it needs to work." Jim started simply with Level Up, using an Excel sheet and a Google Drive folder. "We used free software and basic tools to keep costs down. And that simplicity helped us move fast without overwhelm."

Pia Silva also started with simple systems based on Excel sheets, and still uses Excel sheets for a lot of things, though they've evolved over time. "I've outsourced them to other people who manage them and build them, and can make much more complex systems than mine," she explains. "How they've evolved is that they have a lot more automation and technology in them, so that we can do pretty sophisticated things on a large scale." This is a helpful tip for new entrepreneurs to remember: your systems can grow with your business. Start with a simple, basic system, then add to it and tweak it over time as the needs of your business change.

As far as what things should have systems, Pia's metric is simple: things that are repeatable. As she says, "Every time I have to run a planning session for my community, or coaching calls, or workshops, all of these things have been systematized. That allows me to deliver high value without a lot of input each time. The systems that are most valuable to me personally are ones that support me in executing my part of the business."

The exact places that systems will be most helpful (or necessary) will depend to some extent on your business, its industry, and how you engage with customers. With that said, though, there are some basic systems that just about every business needs.

First and foremost, every business needs to have systems for tracking its finances. Whether it's on a basic spreadsheet or in fancy accounting software doesn't matter, as long as you're accurately recording your expenses and revenue.

There are four other foundational systems I'd recommend for every business to have from the start:

- A client information system, including intake forms, contact details, and communication preferences, and the specifications of their project

- Process documentation, including step-by-step procedures for regular tasks and common scenarios, as well as problem-solving guides

- Information storage, including naming conventions and file organization guidelines, along with access protocols and procedures for updating information

- Communication systems, including how you'll communicate both internally (between team members) and externally (with clients or leads), how you'll track the status of projects, and documentation of major decisions

You can use Pia's standard to decide where your business needs systems. If you do something more than once, it's a task. Once you document it, that becomes a system. Systems are what make the difference between overwhelmed parent entrepreneurs who, say, find themselves sitting in the school parking lot during their kid's basketball game, creating a promotional calendar from scratch (for the hundredth time), and ones who actually make it to the game. Without systems, you waste time trying to remember the right steps for a process, or hunting down passwords and logins, or rewriting the same emails over and over. With systems, you have a playbook that keeps important information and process steps in one accessible place, along with templates you can use for common communications—and, as a result, a lot more time to use for more valuable things.

Another way you can choose which systems your business needs is to start with your pain points. What questions does your team most often ask? What information or details do you struggle to remember? Where do things typically go wrong? Any time you find yourself stressed out or frustrated, take a step back and ask yourself: Would this be easier if I created a system for it? (Spoiler alert: the answer will almost always be "yes").

Remember: you don't have to create all of these systems at once. Start by picking one thing you do repeatedly. If it's a process, write down the steps. If it's a communication, create a template. Save it somewhere you can find it easily and share it with your team if it's something multiple people in the business do. It doesn't need to be complicated. In fact, the simpler, the better. You can always add to it or adjust it as needed down the line.

From this foundation, you can build a system-creating habit. Set aside time specifically for building systems. When your processes change or you discover new pain points, update your systems to reflect them. As your team grows, these initial systems can serve double-duty as training documents. This is the perspective Robert Patin takes. Whenever he's creating a new system, he aims to answer the question: "How do I make it so simple and easy that someone who isn't adept, or doesn't have the knowledge or experience to do the thing, is able to learn from it?" To enhance this learning, he often creates the system in multiple formats. This could include templates, a training video, step-by-step screenshots, and a documented checklist-style SOP version ideal for a quick refresh.

Along with saving you time and streamlining your workflow, creating systems can help you to provide more value to your customers or clients. That was the case for Palak Shah. She initially created systems for her own benefit in her real estate business. "We knew early on that if we didn't systematize the project management and financing process, we'd hit a ceiling fast," she says. "So we documented everything—from deal analysis to contractor selection to refinance timing—and turned it into repeatable workflows. That's how our SCALE Framework was born. It's now the backbone of how we operate our portfolio and how we teach thousands of other investors to do the same."

Systems aren't just valuable for a business, either. They can be just as helpful for making family life easier and smoother. For instance, Pia Silva and her husband use the AnyList app to give the whole family access to a shared grocery list. She also puts easy recipes in there so they can see exactly what ingredients they'll need to make dinner. Mondays and Fridays are designated shopping days, while the house cleaner comes on Thursdays. They also make full use of their calendar, noting days her parents will watch their kid so they get a night to themselves and pre-scheduling vacations to make sure they get taken. "Anything I can do to systematize and automate the things that keep the house running helps give me a little more space and freedom to relax so I can do all of the things I need to do," Pia explains.

For Palak Shah, implementing systems has helped her family simplify. "A lot of families burn out because they're overcommitted," she says. "We operate with intention. That means our systems are built around clarity and capacity. We use shared calendars, aligned routines, and clear roles to keep everything moving efficiently." This supports their goal of deliberately creating a lifestyle that fosters joy and connection, protecting their energy for the things that matter.

Jim Cocks echoes this sentiment, saying, "I treat my family a bit like a team now. There's open communication. We talk about who's low on energy, who needs help, who's sick, and who's stepping up. It's less about perfection and more about understanding each other's capacity and making it work. Bringing in that business mindset—clear roles, empathy, systems—it's made family life smoother, too."

That's really what systems are all about, whether they're in your business or at home: making things easier so you can put your energy toward the things that really matter. And, as Jim said, it's not about being perfect. I still sometimes catch myself defaulting to keeping things in my head. The difference is, now I know better than to rely on memory alone, and I have processes in place to help me resist this temptation. For entrepreneurs who are just getting started, creating your systems now, before you drop an important ball, can help your business run better from the beginning.

Key Takeaways:

- **Get it out of your head and onto paper**: Document key info, processes, and decisions so the biz doesn't live in your brain alone.

- **Create systems early, save sanity later**: Got something you do on repeat? Systemize it from the start. Future you will thank you.

- **Share the knowledge wealth**: Keep your team in the loop so they can fly solo when needed. Bottlenecks are bad for business.

- **Systemize your home life too**: Wrangling a household is no joke. Treat it like a business and watch things run smoother.

CHAPTER 4

Money Truths: Cash Flow, Pricing, and the Mistakes We All Make

Y'all, I touched on financial systems in the last chapter, but we need to dive deeper because money stuff is where most entrepreneurs completely lose their minds. And honestly? It's too important to gloss over.

Let me start with a story about the time my financial chaos almost tanked a big deal. RSG Sales was pitching a major project, and I did what I always did back then: pulled numbers straight out of my ass and called it a day. Pure gut feeling, no real data. What could possibly go wrong, right? I mean, it had always worked before...except, this time, it didn't. I drastically underestimated how many hours our assistant would need to do her part of the project. Of course, I didn't realize this until after the client signed the contract and the price was locked in. Instead of making our usual profit, we ended up losing $500. But here's the thing: that $500 loss was the costly mistake that finally got me to create real money systems, and that was one of the best decisions I've ever made for the business. I can say without hesitation that, if I hadn't developed functional systems to keep track of our expenses and revenue, we never would have been able to scale RSG Sales to the point it's at today.

The good news? You get to learn from my expensive mistake without losing your own grocery money. But before we talk about managing money, we need to address the elephant in the room: where the hell do you get the money to start this thing in the first place? Because let's be real, you need funds not just to launch, but to keep the lights on while you figure out how to make this business actually support your family.

In my experience talking to other entrepreneurs, a sizable percentage of them bootstrapped their launch. By this I mean that they used their own money—either by drawing on their savings or taking out loans or lines of credit—rather than seeking investors. This was the case for all of the entrepreneurs I interviewed in this book. Danielle Ratliff used money from the sale of Serenity Now, her massage business, to fund her marketing agency. When Jim Cocks started Level Up, he was living in his parents' house and driving Uber for income. As he says, "It wasn't glamorous, but it gave me a runway. You don't need a massive investment to start. What you need is your first paying client, and that's all the validation you need to get moving fast. Most people can bootstrap if they're resourceful and driven." Sometimes scrappy is exactly what you need.

Pia Silva started her agency with $3,000 in the bank and made use of lines of credit and interest-free credit cards to supplement this financing. For other founders, she says, "I personally recommend this approach because I've paid very little interest on the money I've used, and I haven't given up any equity or ownership of that money." Smart move. Your business stays yours. Here's what most new entrepreneurs don't realize about investors: they're not doing this out of the kindness of their hearts. They want something back. Either interest payments or a chunk of your company. You need to decide if their money is worth giving up control of your vision.

Now, your family might offer to help fund your dream. Sweet gesture, but proceed with extreme caution. Taking money from family and friends sounds great until it isn't. Suddenly, every family dinner becomes a progress report, and the pressure to succeed becomes crushing. You're not just risking your own money anymore. You're risking relationships with people you actually want to keep around. Business fails, and you lose Aunt Martha's $10K? Good luck at Christmas dinner for the next decade. Yes, some people make family funding work, but I've seen too many relationships implode to recommend it.

Quick reality check: most of the businesses I've mentioned are service-based, which means lower startup costs. Product businesses or anything requiring physical space (like restaurants or salons) need more cash upfront. But don't let that scare you; bootstrapping is still totally possible. You also don't necessarily need to do this alone. Brittany Pickrem started her line of eco-friendly laundry detergent with a partner, with each of them putting in 50% of the required funds. Having a partner means each person shoulders less of the financial risk.

Palak Shah also had a higher financial investment to make when she started her real estate portfolio. She used a mix of financing strategies, combining personal lines of credit and conventional loans with creative leverage. This led to them mastering real estate strategies like BRRRR-style methods and repositioning properties to force appreciation, which proved to be a growth driver in more ways than one. She adapted that financing strategy into a proprietary system, the SCALE Framework, which she turned into a book, *Accelerate Your Real Estate*, expanding her brand and authority for consulting clients. It gave her even more credibility that she'd used that exact system to build her own high-performing, eight-figure portfolio. For other founders, she says, "My advice is to stop thinking like an operator and start thinking like an investor. Use your assets to fund your vision. Don't build your dream business on fumes; build it with runway, optionality, and control." For instance, one part of her financing strategy was to use DSCR-based financing tied to asset performance rather than personal income. That shift gave her the leverage and stability to scale rapidly without overextending.

Bottom line: There are many more ways to fund a business than most people realize. Don't just pick the first option that sounds reasonable. Do your homework. And here's something that'll save your sanity: you don't have to go all-in from day one. Starting as a side hustle while keeping your day job is becoming the norm, not the exception. Yes, this can mean having a lot on your plate during that initial startup phase, especially for parent entrepreneurs, but it dramatically reduces the risk. I've watched friends gradually transition from corporate jobs to full-time business ownership this way, and they're absolutely crushing it now. And if your business doesn't pan out the way you hoped, then you're not left high and dry with no way to support your family. One of the biggest fears for new entrepreneurs, and the fear that stops a lot of people from ever trying.

Okay, so you've figured out how to fund this thing. Now what the hell do you do with that money? Two big pieces of advice here.

First: create a business plan that's actually realistic. And I don't mean some fantasy document that makes you feel good. I mean real research into what this business will actually cost—not just to start, but to keep running. Plan operating costs for at least the first year into your calculations. Most businesses are not profitable in their first year. This doesn't mean that they're failures, simply that it can take time to grow your client base and establish your reputation to the point that the business is sustainable. If you do end up reaching profitability quickly, then great. You can put that money you squirreled away into other things. But if you don't, having extra funds at your disposal will let you keep the business afloat until it does hit that profitability point.

"Business plan" is another of those intimidating phrases that can send people into cold sweats, but it's not as overwhelming as many people think before they start. This doesn't need to be a complicated document. For a small startup, it's basically answering: What are you doing? Who's buying it? How much will it cost? How will you make money? That's it. Don't overthink it.

There are a lot of tools online you can use to help you write a business plan if you feel stuck in a "don't know where to start" kind of paralysis. Unless you plan to seek out loans or investors, the format of the business plan isn't terribly important. What matters is that you've determined whether your business idea is feasible and established the basic guidelines for how you'll approach its early phases.

Second big tip: separate your personal and business money from day one. I'm talking separate bank accounts, separate credit cards, separate everything. Do not—and I cannot stress this enough—do NOT use your business account to buy groceries. If you have multiple business accounts, funnel all deposits into one main account so you can actually see your cash flow without a math degree. Your budgeting should be separate, too, with clear financial targets for each area.

While we're talking money, you need budgets for both sides: business AND personal. Let's start with business. Monitoring your business finances isn't just about how much money comes in. You need to know if you're actually making a profit and whether you're growing or slowly bleeding money. That means identifying which key performance indicators (KPIs) are the most applicable to your business model. You don't need a fancy dashboard, just something that tells you if you're headed in the right direction or off a cliff.

If budgeting makes you want to hide under your desk, relax. You don't need to invent some revolutionary system. I love The Profit First Method by Mike Michalowicz, but there are tons of options. Pick one that doesn't make your brain hurt and stick with it. You also don't need to track your finances manually. Tools like QuickBooks, Mint, and YNAB let you automate your financial recordkeeping, and as an added bonus, they often have built-in tools for things like taxes and payroll.

Let's talk about taxes, because this is where shit gets real and expensive fast. You absolutely must understand the tax rules for your business from day one. I know, I know, taxes are about as fun as a root canal. But ignoring them will cost you.

Here's the thing: generic advice doesn't work. Every business is different, and what worked for your friend's consulting business might be completely wrong for yours. This is something Brittany Pickrem learned the hard way. The conventional wisdom she'd heard was that a business shouldn't incorporate until it's making six-figure yearly revenue. But that advice mostly applies to product-based companies. In Brittany's case, her branding agency is a low-expense, high-margin business, which makes incorporation a smart move at a lower revenue threshold. She also received some bad advice about how much it costs to incorporate. She thought that would be a significant expense until she did a bit of independent research and realized she could incorporate on her own for just a couple of hundred bucks.

"My advice to anybody, if you're a super small business, especially a service-based business, is that you really need to understand how to protect yourself with your taxes. I just listened to something that was a norm, and I should not have done that," Brittany says. In her case, following the typical advice meant she was paying significantly higher taxes than she needed to for the first decade of her business. This didn't only impact her agency's finances. It also prevented her from buying a home and put strain on her personal relationships, which contributed to the end of her marriage. She adds, "What you don't know hurts you the most. It would have changed my life if I had understood tax regulations and rules. It took me ten years to figure it out on my own because I was never given the right guidance or advice."

Once you've got your financial house in order, don't hoard that information. Share it with your team. Create a shared language around the numbers that matter and give regular updates. When people understand how their work impacts the bottom line, they start caring about profitability as much as you do. It's like magic, except it's just good business.

The same wisdom applies to the family side of things. While it's imperative to keep personal and business finances separate, they're still intimately intertwined. The income you make from your business isn't just how you'll survive day-to-day. It's also integral to personal financial goals like saving for retirement, buying a house, investing in your kids' education, or building an emergency fund. Make family financial planning as collaborative as your business planning. Set shared goals and talk about them regularly. Yeah, money conversations can be awkward as hell, but Josh and I getting on the same page financially was one of the best things we ever did for our marriage AND our business.

All of this system's stuff serves one purpose: knowing exactly where you stand financially. That means tracking your net worth (assets minus liabilities), monitoring cash flow (income minus expenses), and spotting problems before they become disasters. When you know where you are, you can figure out where you're going. Without that clarity, you're just guessing. And we've already established how well that works out.

Key Takeaways:

- **Know your numbers like your life depends on it (because it does)**: Get intimate with your revenue, expenses, and profit margins. No excuses.

- **Biz and personal finances are like oil and water**: Keep 'em separated from day one. Trust me on this.

- **Get real with your business plan and budget**: Factor in at least a year of operating costs. Rose-colored glasses have no place here.

- **Don't DIY your taxes**: Work with a small biz accountant who knows their stuff. The IRS is not to be trifled with.

CHAPTER 5

The Right First Hire (Spoiler: It's Still Not Your Friend)

One question I hear constantly from new business owners is, "Who should be my first hire?" They expect me to say something like a salesperson or a virtual assistant. Instead, I usually tell them there's a different question they should ask first: "Am I really ready for employees?"

And honestly, a lot of times, the answer is: not yet.

New entrepreneurs often jump the gun on building a team. This is especially true with service businesses. They over-invest in employees and hire too many people, too early.

Why is this a problem? Good employees don't come cheap. A team that's too big puts serious strain on your cash flow and can take a massive chunk out of your profitability.

I get the mindset that leads to this mistake. Usually, it happens because you're gearing up for a growth spurt and think you'll need more hands on deck to handle the increased workload. Here's the issue, though: if you build a big team first, that means you won't have enough space in your budget to scale up your marketing. That means you can't generate the new leads that would bring in extra business and justify the bigger team you built. What looked like a proactive step to help you grow faster actually ends up killing your momentum.

Jim Cocks has been in this exact situation with Level Up. As he says, "I've definitely made the mistake of hiring too early, thinking more team members would equal more revenue. But unless you've got the demand and systems to support that, it's a drain, not a boost. Entrepreneurs often overlook the fact that their team is their biggest expense. If you hire lean and smart, and use tech well, you can scale without bloating the business."

There's another problem with hiring employees too early: you don't always know what skills you need yet. Robert Patin learned this lesson the hard way. He added a high-level marketing expert to his team early, expecting them to jumpstart his growth. This proved to be a costly mistake.

"I hired the person before I even understood what I wanted from a marketing perspective, and hadn't even learned enough myself to know what questions to be asking," he explains. "I spent a lot of money, and it was a solid six months or so where they completely tanked all of our marketing activity, where things had been working before, and it kind of blew all of that up."

In the end, he had to put in extra effort and money just to get things back to where they'd been before, and he still had to pay the employee while they were on his team, even though they ended up doing more harm than good.

Pia Silva made a similar mistake when she was first growing her consulting business. She was in a situation that probably sounds familiar. She had too much on her plate, and thought hiring would be the solution. In hindsight, she thinks she should've tweaked her systems to be more efficient first and made sure she had the overhead to hire people before she went through with it. In the end, Pia says, "I learned that the solution to running a business wastefully is not to spend more money."

Pia also cautions against hiring sales or marketing team members to compensate for your own lack of skills or knowledge. At one point, she hired a sales team for a program she was launching. "I wanted to outsource the selling because I didn't feel confident enough to sell it myself," she explains. "I learned the expensive way that other people can't sell your stuff until you can sell your stuff. My advice for other entrepreneurs is not to outsource the most important pieces of your business, like sales and marketing, before you've got at least a decent handle on it yourself. Sales and marketing are the lifeblood of your business, and if you don't understand how they work, you're going to have a hard time hiring the right people to execute on them. You're not going to be able to manage those people well because if it doesn't work, you won't know if it's because of them or because of your offer."

This is crucial. If you don't understand the fundamentals of what you're trying to hire for, you'll have no way to evaluate whether someone is doing good work or not.

So when should you hire? Honestly, my experience has been that you should delay it as long as possible. I've made this mistake of hiring too many people too early myself. Now, my approach is to only add team members when something is going to break if we don't. Hiring should be the last step you take to scale, not the first. If there's any other way to expand your capacity, like adding a new tool or creating a new system, you should do that before you hire.

I know this probably isn't what you wanted to hear if you're currently in a situation like Pia was, where you feel completely overwhelmed by everything on your plate. I'm going to tell you something now that might surprise you, but hear me out.

Your first hire as a parent entrepreneur shouldn't be for your business at all. It should be someone to clean your house.

As both a business owner and a parent, your time and energy are constantly being drained. It's that non-stop stacking of responsibilities that leads to feeling overwhelmed, and that stack shrinks when you outsource household tasks lurking at the bottom of your to-do list. Nothing sucks the creative life force out of you quite like scrubbing toilets when you should be closing sales.

It's easy to find someone who can clean your bathroom as well as you can. Finding someone you trust to manage your sales or represent your business to clients is a much taller order. That person is going to take longer to find, require more training and oversight, and cost more once you've brought them on board. Eventually, it will be worth it to find that superstar sales representative. In the early stages of a business, though, the mental space that opens up once you no longer have "clean bathrooms" on your permanent to-do list is priceless. It's giving yourself permission to focus on what actually matters.

Outsourcing things off your personal to-do list doesn't always need to mean hiring a professional. Getting the whole family involved in household chores can be a lifesaver as a parent entrepreneur, whether that's teaching everyone over the age of 8 to use the washing machine or splitting dinner prep duties between you and your partner. You can also lean on your community. Getting help with yard work doesn't need to mean hiring a professional landscaper. The teenager who lives down the street might be happy to mow your lawn or weed your garden for a rate that doesn't break a tight budget.

The important thing isn't who you delegate tasks to. It's the mindset shift, giving yourself permission to not do it all. Moms especially often deal with guilt about needing help, like that means you've somehow failed at being Superwoman. Newsflash: Superwoman is fictional, and even she didn't own a business while raising humans. Outsourcing isn't admitting defeat. It's being smart about how you manage your resources. Your time and mental energy are valuable, and there's no point in wasting them on things that really aren't important.

This same logic can apply within your business, too. Bringing on help doesn't always mean hiring employees. Brittany Pickrem has no desire to hire a team for her branding agency, but that doesn't mean she does everything herself. She turns to freelancers and other entrepreneurs. By this point, she says, "I have a roster of talent. I have a layout designer, I have a web designer, I have a copywriter…I expand my team based on whatever my clients' needs are, and I stay in my own lane. That keeps me focused on the expertise that I bring, but I bring people on as I need them. I don't want the stress of employees."

Freelancers may cost more per hour than an employee in straight salary, but they're still usually more cost-effective overall for a small business. For one thing, you don't need to pay them all the time, only when you have work for them. You also skip the other costs associated with employees, like benefits, payroll taxes, and insurance. The trick is to be thoughtful about which work you outsource. The best tasks for freelancers are ones that are time-consuming but necessary, can't be easily automated, and are in areas where you don't have skills or find joy. The things you don't want to outsource are core tasks that are critical to your business.

Jim Cocks seconds this suggestion. The biggest mistake he's made with his business, he says, was "throwing money at problems I didn't want to face, or trying to shortcut my way out of a situation I wasn't ready to handle. I've hired agencies to fix lead gen or sales, thinking it would be a quick win, and it wasn't. What I've learned is that no one will ever care about your business as much as you do. Unless there's a really strong mutual interest, agencies are rarely fully invested in your success. Now, I steer away from outsourcing anything critical to strangers."

One last topic we should talk about is the temptation to hire friends or family. This is one of those things that looks like a good idea in theory. I know this because this is a mistake that I've made more than once. I suck at hiring people. Truly, I do. And I've made one mistake repeatedly that cost me not just money and time, but something far more valuable: friendships. Every time, it seemed like a perfect match at first. I have a friend who needs a job right when I need help in the business, so why not help both of us out? You know them, so you don't need to waste time interviewing, and they might even be willing to work for less than you'd pay a stranger.

But that's actually part of the problem. There aren't built-in boundary lines with your friends or relatives like there are with employees. If you get drinks after work, are you buddies or boss and coworker? If you text them with work stuff on the weekends, are they allowed to ignore it? Friends might also expect special treatment like extra flexibility with deadlines, more input into business decisions, or more leeway when they make mistakes. On the other side, you might expect more loyalty or willingness to put in extra time or effort. These expectations are usually unspoken on both sides, and may even be subconscious, but that doesn't stop them from hurting people's feelings when they're not met.

It's much harder to be a good boss to people you know from your personal life. Giving constructive feedback feels awkward, which can often mean they just don't get any, or you sugar-coat things, or, worst of all, that you bottle your frustration up until you explode. Conversations about pay are more awkward, too, especially if they know details of your business finances that make them feel undervalued. Then, when you do have disagreements, the ripples impact your personal life. Others in your circle feel the need to take sides, and there's a new, uncomfortable dimension to family gatherings and social outings. Trust me, you don't want to have to spend Thanksgiving dinner explaining to your mom why you had to fire your cousin or your sister.

The bottom line is, every single time that I've hired a friend or relative, it's gone terribly wrong. Inevitably, we've had a conflict that didn't just result in them leaving the business but also soured our relationship. I'm definitely not the only one who has had this experience, either. When I asked other entrepreneurs how they felt about hiring friends and relatives, their answer was nearly across the board: don't do it.

Jade Green isn't just a business owner but also a recruitment expert, giving her extra insight into this kind of question. Her advice is, "Don't hire friends, family, or fools. You need to hire the right person for the right role. And more often than not, hiring friends leads to blurred lines, broken boundaries, and messy expectations. With family, you end up giving special permissions or tolerating things you wouldn't with anyone else, and that dynamic makes it really hard to lead effectively or hold accountability." She does give the caveat that if your friend or relative is genuinely the best person for the job, and has gone through the same interview process as a stranger, then it might be okay, but even then, she says, "You need to be hyper aware. Hold your boundaries. Lead with clarity."

Nick Rodsater is one of the rare entrepreneurs who has successfully worked with family members at his chiropractic practice. The big difference in this case, though, is that Aligning the World is a family business. He and his wife met in chiropractic school and opened their practice together. Their children have worked in the business, and so has his sister. Nick appreciates working with family because, as he says, "We will never have other employees who are more bought in to what we do than our family." He agrees with the other founders I spoke to about the need for firm boundaries, though, saying, "The one thing that I did learn when we hired my sister was to make sure that we set clear expectations and didn't let any outside stuff cloud how we communicate." Nick would be open to working with friends, as well, though he stipulates, "It would all have to start with making sure that our values and vision were aligned, and then we would need to establish clear objectives around how we handle the relationship within the business and outside the business."

In this regard, our situation at RSG Sales is similar to Nick's. Josh and I started the business together, and our kids have worked in our businesses at various points. The reason this has worked, though, is the same thing those other founders mentioned: we established clear roles that suited each of our strengths. Palak Shah and her husband also work on most of their businesses together, and she believes that the integration of their business into their family has strengthened their relationship. Even so, she says, "It's not easy to work with your spouse. But it's also been rewarding and transformative. Working together has forced us to grow individually and as a unit. We learned how to communicate better, how to resolve conflict in real time, and how to respect each other's strengths and do everything in our power to help the other person succeed. Perhaps most importantly, it's allowed us to model true partnership for our children. They get to see what collaboration looks like. They see the passion, the challenges, the wins, and they see us navigating it all together. That's a legacy in itself."

While you can find more examples of spouses who are successful co-owners, even this isn't guaranteed to succeed if the roles and people aren't a good fit. For instance, Pia Silva built her agency with her husband, Steve, and, because they had clear roles, that worked for a long time. But, she says, "When it all started to go sideways was when we hired our first two employees. There were a lot of roles and domains for which it was unclear who was responsible. It took us a couple of years to realize how important it was to neatly clarify who was responsible for what." Ultimately, when the opportunity came up for Pia to start a new business and Steve to pivot to a career as an artist, they both embraced it. As Pia says, "I was really excited and ready to have my own business without a partner so that I could do it exactly the way I wanted."

The same was true for Robert Patin and his husband, Tom. They started their business together, but that ended up putting Tom in a career that he didn't really want. By this point, he's mostly pulled back from the business, and both the company and their marriage are better for it. As for hiring other family members, Robert says, "Absolutely not, I will never do it again." He's hired several relatives and had one work out well, but the rest "left in a pretty dramatic, explosive fashion."

The bottom line here is that every person you bring into the business should be there for a reason. You should truly believe they're the best ones for the job and establish clear responsibilities and expectations for them, whether or not you knew each other before their interview. And before you hire anyone, take a step back to make absolutely sure that you're ready for that step. Hiring too early and hiring the wrong people are two of the most common mistakes new business owners make, and either one can cause serious problems that go well beyond the scope of that role.

Key Takeaways:

- **Delay hiring as long as possible**: Only add team members when something will break without them. Try tools and systems first. Hiring is your last step to scale, not first.

- **Your first hire? Clean your house**: Scrubbing toilets at midnight drains more creative energy than anything else. Free up mental space for what actually matters.

- **Never hire friends or family**: I've lost friendships every time. Boundary lines blur, and someone always gets hurt. Just don't.

- **Master it before you delegate it**: Don't outsource sales or marketing until you can do it yourself. Otherwise, you won't know if failure is theirs or your offer.

CHAPTER 6

Taming the Chaos: Time, Energy, and the Truth About Busy

I can tell you the exact moment I realized I needed to take control of my time. It was 2013, when I was first starting E by Design, and I was in peak overwhelmed-entrepreneur-mom form. Not only did I now have two businesses to run, but I was also President of the PTA, Team Mom for two of my kids' basketball teams, and, in between all that, trying to fit in time to volunteer at church and be present for my husband and parents. I had hit a point where I always felt behind, even though I worked all the time, as in "taking client calls from the school pickup line" and "laptop open while waiting for the basketball game to start" kind of always on. It was inevitable that I was going to hit rock bottom sooner rather than later, even if I was too deep in the weeds to realize it.

It was a comment from the Head of the Upper School that helped me regain some perspective. At the time, my solution to my overwhelming to-do list was to sleep four hours a night and use the wee hours of the morning to catch up on my email—and yes, I realize in hindsight that this was absolutely not sustainable, or even realistically functional, but that was where my brain was at the time. I had sent the Head of the Upper School an email about an upcoming PTA event at 3 a.m., during one of these so-early-it's-late email sessions. The next time we had a meeting, he looked at me and said, "Heather, what in the world are you doing emailing about PTA stuff at 3 a.m.? It's not life or death."

Once I got over my mortification at being called out, I realized that he was completely right. There was no reason I should be doing anything but sleeping at 3 a.m. I had to figure out a way to manage my time more effectively. For me, the strategy that actually worked, when nothing else I had tried seemed to do the trick, was time blocking.

If your reaction to that phrase is an automatic eye roll, I get it. No, time blocking isn't the "instantly crush your goals" hack that some business bloggers make it out to be. But it is a super useful tool to wrangle an overloaded schedule. Many people think time blocking means scheduling every second of your day to cram as much into it as possible, but that's not what it's really about. The real magic of time blocking is that it gives you permission to focus on one thing at a time. When you do that, your brain isn't constantly task-switching, which is exhausting and leads to everything taking longer than it needs to. You also stop wasting energy feeling guilty about what you're not doing and can be fully present and focused on whatever block you're currently in, whether that's putting in some deep work for a client's project or spending time with your kids. In short, time blocking can bring order to the chaos of running a business while raising humans.

The first step to time blocking the right way is to do a quick reality check. Identify your non-negotiables—the things that you need to prioritize, no matter what—and be honest about them. For me, this was a fairly standard list: client commitments and team meetings on the work side; kid activities, school drop-offs and pickups, and time with Josh on the family side; and exercise for my own health and sanity. These are my anchors that everything else flows around.

Once you've identified your anchors, you can start to schedule focus blocks. These are blocks of roughly 90 minutes when you're at your best, and you can schedule your highest value work. When the kids were in school, for instance, this was 11 a.m.–1:30 p.m.: after I'd dropped the kids off and knocked out a couple of chores, but before my energy reserves ran low. This may not be the only focus block in a given day, but it's when I know I do my best thinking, so it's the core one I schedule other things around.

Another tip I'll share from experience is not to schedule your blocks immediately back-to-back. I add a 15–30 minute buffer between them. This was another game-changer when I discovered this tweak. The first reason is that, no matter how thoughtfully you create your schedule, life happens. A sick kid or client emergency can torpedo your day when you have every minute from waking to sleeping slotted into a block. A buffer gives you room to absorb the unexpected. On those rare smooth days, you can use this buffer time to give your mind a rest, take a walk, or do some breathing exercises—something that keeps you calm and in the zone during your next block.

This buffer time can also help you avoid a common mistake with time blocking, and one that I regularly made when I started doing it: over-scheduling. For some reason, I would act like blocking time meant I could fit 8 hours of work into a 6-hour school day. Time blocking might feel like magic, but it's not. You still need to be realistic about how long each task will take. You'll likely have some trial-and-error at first while you discover how much time you actually need for certain tasks, but the more you practice this technique, the more accurate you'll get with slotting items into the appropriate block length.

To give you an idea of what a time-blocked day might look like in real life, here's an example of my morning blocks when my kids were younger:

- 5:00–6:45 a.m. Self-Care block: This would be my time to wake up and get in some quick exercise like yoga or a run.

- 7:00–8:30 a.m. Morning power block: This would include the day's first quick email check, along with getting the kids ready and off to school.

- 9:30–11:00 a.m. Team block: I'd start the work day by checking in with my teams and reviewing our current projects. This is also when I would ideally schedule any meetings.

- 11:00–11:30 a.m. Buffer: Time to make any needed schedule adjustments or send responses to urgent emails or messages.

- 11:30 a.m.–1:00 p.m. Focus block: My key time of the day for deep work on client projects or business strategy planning.

That focus block would be followed by another 30-minute buffer before I'd move into my afternoon, breaking the day up into similar blocks like the ones above. Notice that none of the blocks run right into each other. Even if it's just a little 15-minute break, I always make a point of leaving time for life to happen.

This is just an example of how I structured my days. You definitely don't need to use the same blocks or put them in the same order. Time blocking works best when it follows your natural rhythms. Robert Patin is a fellow time-blocker, and he likes to start his day with the most important task, explaining, "That's where I focus my time first thing in the morning when I have my brain on the most." Every Thursday, he looks ahead at his time blocks for two weeks, refining his blocks for the week that's coming up and scheduling his blocks for the one after that. He also uses these blocks as a way to get more clarity into how he's using his time overall. Once a quarter, he'll go through his time data and look for the things he's devoting time to that are the least valuable or no longer serving the business. Then, he'll decide what new tasks need to be added to his list to grow his company, and slot those in place of those low-value tasks.

One challenge for me when I first started time blocking was actually focusing only on the one task I had assigned to each block. Sometimes I'd break in the middle of the block for "just a quick email check" before getting back to what I should be doing. Here's the thing: these things I'd tell myself would only take a couple of minutes could easily stretch to fill up the rest of the block, throwing off my entire plan. Time blocking can only be successful if you stick to your schedule. Those emails will still be there when the block ends, so wait to think about them until then. If you do slip up, or if an emergency in your family or business blows up your carefully scheduled day, don't let that stress you out. It's not about perfect execution. Time blocking is a tool to help you manage your time, not a rule you need to feel compelled to follow. Try to avoid the all-or-nothing mindset. If today's blocks get disrupted, just reset and try again tomorrow.

To be honest, the singular focus aspect of time blocking is more important than how you schedule things. Pia Silva's time management strategy uses a similar concept but in a slightly different way. She has firm boundaries around her workday and breaks projects into chunks that she slots into her calendar, with the goal of focusing on one project at a time. The difference is that she leaves some of her work days completely open. "That allows me to have chunks of time available for the bigger projects that I need to work on," she explains. "For example, I might spend an entire morning just creating my LinkedIn content, or videos, or strategizing a new lesson for my clients. And that's very flexible because those are the kinds of projects that I can do at any time, and there's not a real time crunch on it."

Now, here's another strategy that works hand in hand with time blocking: The Pomodoro method. This strategy centers on working in focused 25-minute sprints, followed by short breaks. In a sense, it's a condensed time blocking approach, and one that can be a perfect fit for parent entrepreneurs. It's much easier to find 25 free minutes in a hectic day than it is to schedule a full 90. You can fit one Pomodoro between school drop-off and your day's first meeting, for instance, or get through two while your kid is at basketball practice (or whatever after-school activity they have going on). The point is, even when life feels like straight chaos, anyone can hold focus for 25 minutes, and you won't need to reorganize your entire life to fit these blocks in. The breaks in between them can help to prevent burnout and keep your mind sharp when you're in a sprint. Using this approach can also help overcome decision fatigue because you don't need to wonder what to work on next. Every Pomodoro is devoted to a single task, so you're not wasting mental energy on task-switching.

Just like with time blocking, you want to view the Pomodoro approach as a tool rather than a hard-and-fast rule. The 25-minute length is perfect for me, but you can adjust that up to 35 minutes if it takes you a few minutes to get into the zone, or even drop it down to 20 if that's all the time you have to work with. The length of the breaks between sprints can be tweaked, too. Sometimes, the break might be a task instead of a specific amount of time—for me, that "break" sometimes was driving to school pickup. As long as you're still giving your brain a rest, how you use that time is up to you.

Here's something I discovered that might surprise you: time-blocking and the Pomodoro method aren't either/or strategies. They actually stack beautifully together. Three 25-minute sprints, each followed by a 5-minute break, fit perfectly into a 90-minute time block. When you have several short but important things to accomplish in a day, using this combination method gives you a truly deep focus on them and helps to maximize your productivity.

Just like with time blocking, the trick to using the Pomodoro technique effectively is to limit all distractions and focus just on that one task. If you're like me, you'll suddenly remember everything else you need to do as soon as you start a Pomodoro. I keep a scratch pad on my desk so I can jot them down and keep going. Once I'm on my break between sprints, I'll review the notepad and slot those tasks into my schedule. It also helps to turn off all notifications, close your email inbox, and put your phone on Do Not Disturb so you don't have digital distractions breaking your focus.

Once you start using these strategies, you might find some surprising ways to apply them. I like to use the Pomodoro Method for meetings, for example. It keeps everyone on track when you know you have to get through the whole agenda in 25 minutes. It also catches people's attention when you schedule a meeting for 25 minutes instead of 30. This small detail sends a message that you want to make every minute of the meeting count.

The goal with both of these strategies isn't to turn yourself into a productivity robot. Really, they're about giving yourself permission to focus on one thing at a time, guilt-free, while also inserting natural break points between tasks that keep your brain fresh and stave off burnout. For entrepreneurs trying to manage their time in the real world, that is worth its weight in gold (or coffee, or tea—whatever is your most valuable resource). If the idea of scheduling your whole day feels overwhelming, start small. Commit to doing one Pomodoro a day for a week, then expand from there until you find a scheduling strategy that works for your brain and life.

Key Takeaways:

- **Establish clear "work" and "home" zones**: Set rules about when shop talk is allowed. Hint: not at the dinner table or before coffee.

- **Redistribute the housework deck**: Your role is changing, so your partner's and kids' needs to as well. It takes a village.

- **Design a biz that supports your life, not consumes it**: Your business should serve your lifestyle, not the other way around.

CHAPTER 7

Time Boundaries for Founders (Because No One Else Will Set Them For You)

If you're an entrepreneur, you've probably heard something along the lines of, "It's 6:30 a.m. You want to talk about the business now?" Or maybe you were the one saying this if you work with your spouse and their business brain doesn't have an off switch. The point is, when you're a business owner, it can feel like all you do is eat, breathe, and sleep your business, especially in those early days of a new company. You end up thinking about it at the most inopportune times: during family dinner, when you're trying to fall asleep, or before you've even had your first sip of coffee (or tea) in the morning.

If you relate to this problem, you're definitely not alone. The work of building a business from scratch can't always be wrangled into a neat 9–5 workday. You might find yourself putting in 12-hour days or replying to client emails during the intermission of your kid's recital. The problem is, if you're not careful, that occasional long day can morph into your business taking over your life. When you don't feel like you can ever step away, that's when burnout becomes a very real threat, and you stop bringing your best self to either side of your life.

Here's something that might surprise you about entrepreneurship, and something that caught Jim Cocks off guard when he first started Level Up. In those early days, "your business really does take over your life. You'll work weekends, give up social events, and probably burn out more than once. It can affect your relationships, your social circle, everything." I've seen this pattern with so many entrepreneurs, and I certainly lived it myself in those first years of RSG Sales.

But here's what Jim taught me that I wish I'd known earlier: it doesn't stay that way forever. "Once you build the right team, create solid systems, and get some momentum, it starts to feel lighter. The long-term reward is freedom and flexibility. But you have to be willing to get through that short-term hustle and grind phase first." The key is surviving those early years without burning out to the point where you want to just give up and walk away.

That's where boundaries become your lifeline. Josh and I saved our sanity by setting what we call our 8-to-7 rule: No work talk before 8 a.m. or after 7 p.m. Do we always follow this rule perfectly? Definitely not. We've each had our share of "it popped into my head and out of my mouth" moments outside of work hours. Part of this is just human nature. We're both passionate about our business, so it's not always easy to stop thinking about it, especially when something big or stressful is happening, like a major client issue, a challenging decision, or a major growth opportunity. But, by at least having the rule, it's something the other person can point to when they need a mental break.

What I've discovered is that when we do fall off the boundary wagon, and work starts taking over, it only makes me more stressed and anxious. Our business is important, yes, but it's not the only important thing in our lives, and that's crucial to remember as a parent entrepreneur. Establishing boundaries doesn't mean you care less about your business; it's actually the opposite: you need boundaries because you care so much. Your brain needs downtime to process, integrate, and rejuvenate. Constantly thinking about your business doesn't lead to better results. It leads to burnout and diminished creativity. When we hold to our boundaries, we have more productive work conversations and more quality family time. I also get better sleep, and there's less business-related tension in our relationship, both things that make it easier to think creatively and collaborate when it *is* time to focus on growing RSG Sales.

Even when the business does need extra time, you can set boundaries around how much it takes up. When something big needs attention during the evening or over the weekend, we set a specific "work date" to talk about it. We've also come up with some other strategies that pair with our 8-to-7 rule and help us maintain some semblance of balance. First, we have a spot in our house that's the official "business conversation zone." If one of us has a non-urgent business thought outside of work hours, we write it down and either save it for when we're both in that space or bring it up the next day. We also keep a shared note where we can quickly jot down thoughts that come up in off-hours. This gets the idea out of my or Josh's head, without it launching a full business discussion when we should be thinking about other things. Our last little trick is a code word that either of us can use when the other slips into business talk. This is a gentler way to maintain those time boundaries than a frustrated, "Can we please not talk about work right now?"

Whether your spouse is involved in your business or not, if you're an entrepreneur who's also managing caretaking or household responsibilities, starting a business means you need to establish new boundaries and shift some of those responsibilities. If you don't, you'll be on the fast track into what I call Scorecard Syndrome. That mental state where you tally up all your tasks for the day against what your partner has (or hasn't) done, calculations that almost always leave you feeling resentful, underappreciated, and most of all exhausted.

Let me share my experience with this, because it might sound familiar. Becoming an entrepreneur was a serious role shift for me. Before we started the business, I was a stay-at-home parent for 12 years. This meant I did the heavy lifting when it came to raising the kids, housework, yard work, paying bills, scheduling appointments, you name it, I was the one who did things for the house and family by default. This was completely unsustainable once I was also working full-time, but by that point, Josh and I had been married for just over 14 years, and we'd gotten into deeply entrenched habits when it came to how we split up household labor. In hindsight, it was unrealistic to expect Josh to automatically know he should pick up 50% of those tasks. I also admit I did a terrible job of explaining my expectations.

This didn't lead to a single dramatic breaking point. Instead, it was a thousand tiny moments where I felt like I was being pulled in every direction, none of which were getting the results I wanted. After years of frustration, I finally found an approach that moved me from resentment and overwhelm to resolution and balance.

The first step was a mindset reset. I had to shift my thinking when it came to outsourcing tasks. Adding entrepreneurship to an already full to-do list was simply not sustainable. Shifting some of those tasks to other people wasn't giving up or failing; it was a necessity of our new reality that honored my strengths while acknowledging my limitations. Pia Silva and I have compared notes and commiserated about our own journeys. For Pia, her work-life balance got dramatically better when her husband started handling a lot of the house responsibilities, like getting their son ready for school and taking care of their food. He's a full-time artist with a much more flexible schedule than her business, and that shift gave her the time and space she needed to focus on what she does best.

But here's something I learned the hard way: this approach isn't going to work for everyone. In our case, shifting things from my plate to Josh's simply wasn't working smoothly. My lesson for you is one I wish someone had told me earlier: in a partnership where one person has been handling certain responsibilities for years, expecting a sudden shift to 50/50 is setting yourself up for disappointment and massive failure. It's not a matter of willingness. It's about awareness, skills, and habits that have been developed over time. Your partner might genuinely want to help, but they lack the know-how and systems that you've refined through repetition.

So I found another solution: hiring people to clean the house and take care of the yard. I know not everyone has space in their budget for hired help, especially if you're bootstrapping a new business that's not bringing in much profit yet. If that's your situation, I have two pieces of advice. First, simplify as much as possible. Can bills be put on autopayments so you don't have to think about them? Could you do all of your meal prep for the week at once to save time on a day-to-day basis? Look for ways that tasks could be combined, automated, or eliminated to free up space in your schedule.

My second piece of advice is to look at all of the tasks for the household and redistribute them across the entire family based on skills and preferences, not predefined roles. For parents, this could mean assigning age-appropriate chores to the kids or having family clean-up times where everyone helps to fold the laundry, do the dishes, or declutter. Creating quick checklists or systems that anyone can follow will overcome the "but I don't know how" objection. It might take some time for everyone to get on board with the new routines. Stay patient and focus on communicating clearly, making specific requests when tasks aren't completed, and expressing your expectations without making accusations. It helps if you can build accountability into your systems so that they don't require nagging. Tie kids' allowances to chores, for instance. This can be an excellent way to motivate them to contribute.

Something I've learned from talking to other entrepreneurs is that freedom doesn't just come automatically with business ownership. Palak Shah put it perfectly when she told me, "I thought entrepreneurship would give me freedom by default. But freedom is something you have to design. It doesn't come from owning a business. It comes from owning your decisions. Your boundaries. Your model." She's absolutely right. Entrepreneurship can give you everything you want, or it can trap you worse than a job. The difference is whether you build your business around your life or your life around your business.

For Palak, the whole reason she left a 6-figure corporate job was to get freedom to spend time with her family, and she's designed her business with this in mind by building a strong team, investing in income-producing assets, and having clear systems. What I love about her approach is that she doesn't confuse working hard with being trapped. As she told me, "That doesn't mean I don't work hard. I absolutely do—but I do it on my terms."

This idea of designing your freedom on your own terms is something I see in successful entrepreneurs over and over again. Pia Silva maintains balance by sticking to her intentions, both short-term and long-term. On a day-to-day basis, she makes it a point to schedule time for exercise every morning when she wakes up. She told me something that really stuck with me: "I don't actually exercise every single morning of the week, but that's my intention, and I end up exercising four to six times a week because of it." Even if she wakes up and doesn't feel great, she'll still go down to the gym to stretch and often finds that she ends up exercising once she's there. But even if she doesn't, it sets the tone that she takes care of herself and has time for herself. She also sticks to her schedule of not working nights and weekends.

On the bigger picture level, Pia does something brilliant: she has a planning day at the start of every year where she schedules all of their family trips, couples trips, and solo trips into her calendar first. She also buys any plane tickets right then and there, so she stays committed to taking the trip. Pia takes the months of July and August to focus on fun and family time. During those break times, she might work a couple of days a week, but it's only what she absolutely has to show up for. What I learned from her is the importance of prioritizing work-life balance by being really clear about what your ideal life looks like. Plan that life into your schedule first, then let work fill in the gaps after—instead of the other way around.

As someone in the healthcare field, Nick Rodsater understands better than most how important it is to prioritize health when you're running a business. He has several techniques he uses to manage stress, from positive affirmations and breathing techniques to eating well and getting regular chiropractic care. But what impressed me most about his approach is how intentional he is about family time. As he told me, "I always value time with my family and try to get my mental state away from the business on a weekly basis. We have worked hard to figure out how much time our kids need from us and how much time we truly need with them to feel like our buckets are being filled up and not running out." Once they figured out what that looked like, they worked hard to schedule that time in, whether it's breakfast twice a week or making time to play catch.

The bottom line with all of this is that, as an entrepreneur, you can't expect work and life to just magically sort themselves out in your schedule. It takes intentional planning, and how you handle responsibilities at home can have as much of an impact as the boundaries you set around work.

There's no magic formula here. Everyone's life is different, and what works for someone else might be a disaster for you. As your business grows and your life evolves, your approach to finding balance is probably going to change, too. But the core idea stays the same: understand what the important things are that you need to make time for, and which things aren't important or don't need your full attention. When you're designing systems to manage your time, base them on your actual life right now (not what you think it is or should be), and what will make your current reality easier. You probably won't get it perfect right away, but every step you take toward finding that balance will give you back some of your time and energy so that your home life and business can both thrive.

Key Takeaways:

- **Block time for your top to-dos**: Build in buffers for curveballs. They're gonna happen, so leave room for 'em.

- **Pomodoro that ish**: Focused work sprints are where the magic happens. Set a timer and watch your productivity soar.

- **Tackle the homefront on weekends**: A little meal prep and chore catch-up on Sundays means less Monday mayhem. You're welcome.

CHAPTER 8

Why Good Advice Can Still Lead to Bad Decisions

Let's be clear here: you will make mistakes when you're starting a new business.

Period.

There's no avoiding it. Having said that, you can still save yourself a lot of time, money, and headaches by avoiding them when you can, and knowing the common mistakes people make is the first step in doing that. I talked about some of them in the chapters you've already read. But there are a lot of mistakes waiting to trip up new entrepreneurs, and most people make more than one (sometimes multiple times) in the process of building their business.

One of the annoying things about business mistakes is that you can make them even when you're following expert advice. Brittany Pickrem's experience with taxes in Chapter 4 is an example of this. Following conventional wisdom led her to make a very expensive mistake for years until she realized she could do things a different way. It's important to remember that every entrepreneur and business is unique, and even experts don't always have all the answers.

Now, this doesn't mean you should go to the other extreme and ignore all advice. It's a balancing act that I've seen a lot of entrepreneurs struggle with. Robert Patin learned this the hard way and shared something with me that really stuck: "Don't try to do it alone. Talk to other people. The number one thing that hindered my own growth was thinking that I should be smart enough to do it entirely on my own." He's absolutely right. You can figure most things out yourself, but do you really want to spend years doing what someone else could teach you in months?

But here's the other side of that coin: not everything people tell you is something you should actually do. Robert put it perfectly: you need to take the pieces that work for you and discard the rest, but make sure you're being truly thoughtful about it. Don't just dismiss advice because it sounds hard or different from what you want to hear.

Jim Cocks agrees completely. As he told me, "Just because someone else is doing something doesn't mean it's right for you." This is so important to remember. You can learn from others and still make decisions that are right for your specific situation.

I've mentioned a few times already that it's helpful to have a business mentor, but I should give the caveat that not just any mentor will do. You want to find someone who's the right fit for you and your business, and that can be tricky when you're still figuring out exactly what your business is and what your goals are for it. This is the main reason new entrepreneurs fall into what I call the Guru Trap, where they invest in coaching that isn't just unhelpful but can actively hurt their growth.

This is a pattern I've seen more often as the guru industry has blown up in recent years. It seems like everywhere you turn these days, there's someone promising to help you "build a seven-figure coaching business" or "scale to six figures"—assuming you pay them a few thousand dollars first. Not all of these coaches are predatory (though some are). Some are legitimately valuable programs for the right kind of business in the right market. The problem is, even a well-designed program will be a waste of money if it's not a match for your industry, audience, and personality.

I've learned this lesson about mentor fit from watching Jim Cocks navigate a really expensive mistake. He was part of a coaching program that advised him to break his high-ticket $15,000-plus programs into tiny weekly payments. The coach probably meant well, but this approach was completely wrong for Level Up. Jim ended up with horrible cash flow, constant debt collection issues, and clients who weren't committed because they weren't investing enough to really care about the results.

Fortunately, Jim was smart enough to recognize the problem and reverse course. When he raised his prices back up and eliminated those low-ball payment plans, everything changed. His clients got better results because they showed up differently. As Jim learned, when you charge a premium, your clients value the work more—and they actually succeed more because of it.

Based on my own experiences and conversations with other founders, I've identified some red flags of guru traps. The biggest one is whether they guarantee results. Anyone who promises specific financial outcomes is selling a fantasy, not a business strategy. Ethical business educators talk in terms of frameworks and principles, not guaranteed dollar amounts.

In a similar vein, if they only show success stories but never mention what percentage of students see those results, that's a definite warning sign. You should also be wary if you can't clearly understand what you'll learn before you pay, or if their marketing focuses more on the teacher's high-end lifestyle than the content of the course. Vague promises of "transformational systems" don't cut it. They should be specific about their methods and strategies up front.

Finally, steer clear of programs that pressure you to decide quickly or dismiss your questions or concerns, especially if they do it in a manipulative way, like saying you're "not ready for success" if you won't buy in blindly. Good teachers welcome thoughtful questions and should be equally as selective in who they take on as students as you are about who you choose as a mentor.

So how do you find genuine business guidance without falling into expensive traps?

The first step is to seek out results that make sense for your business stage. If you just launched a month ago, joining a "scale to seven figures" program is trying to run before you learn to walk. Instead, look for mentors who can help you create foundational systems or secure your first few clients.

Along with matching your stage, the teacher's experience should align with your business model and goals. Even a successful course creator might not be the best guide for someone starting a photography studio— it's a completely different business and customer base, and needs different strategies to succeed. Look for someone who has found real success running the same kind of business that you're building. Ideally, you should also get a taste for their teaching style before you go all-in.

Before I enrolled in a business coaching program, I attended a conference where the coach was the keynote speaker, as well as an event that her team hosted. This let me see her teaching style and philosophy before I made a big investment. Taking this kind of methodical approach to selecting a mentor can absolutely make the difference between a valuable investment and an expensive mistake.

One of the hardest lessons I've learned from talking to entrepreneurs like Jade Green is why due diligence matters so much when you're choosing investors or partners. Jade's story really opened my eyes to this. About three years into her business, she was planning to shift from recruitment to culture consulting. Then this group of highly sought-after investors approached her with what seemed like an amazing opportunity; not just cash, but high-level strategic support. The catch? She had to keep the business focused on recruitment.

What Jade didn't realize at the time was that she needed to look much more closely at their track record. She didn't put the right protective clauses in place either. The result? Most of that leadership team disappeared on the day of the transaction. She had genuinely believed that bringing in five big-name heavy-hitters from different industries would be game-changing. Instead, four of them were gone before they even got started.

But what I really admire about Jade is that she learned from this experience and applied it right away. Recently, when she was preparing for a joint venture with one of her clients, she realized it wasn't a good fit and pulled out of the project. As she told me, "Unless you really know someone, you need time, space, and an honest connection to see their personal values, ethics, and how they actually live. Because a business partnership is more of a commitment than a romantic one."

Here's something else I've learned from watching entrepreneurs like Jade: you need to have the confidence and self-awareness to know when it's time to cut your losses. This is true whether it means dropping out of a poor-fit coaching program, pulling out of a partnership deal, eliminating a product or service that isn't selling, or even stepping away from the business entirely. This can be a very difficult decision to make. When you've put a lot of time or money into something, it can be soul-crushing to have to scrap those plans and feel like it was all a waste. There's actually a name for this: the sunk-cost fallacy, where people resist giving up on something they've heavily invested in even when it's obvious to everyone else that walking away is the better choice.

The fear of failure definitely plays into this when it comes to entrepreneurship. When you've built something from scratch on your own, it can feel like a personal failure when it doesn't work out. It's especially painful when you look at other entrepreneurs on social media who are thriving with the same kind of business you're struggling to build. This is where it can actually be helpful to remember that most startups fail; roughly 90% of them within their first 5 years, according to recent statistics from Forbes. These stats aren't particularly heartening to look at most of the time, but they do help you to stay grounded in reality. If you need to close your business and try again, you're definitely not alone, and letting go of that first venture when it's time can clear the way for something that will be successful. One thing I often say to people: "It's only money." Yes, it can be a lot of money; it certainly hurt to write off my start-up investment into Sercy as a loss when I closed that business. But that first business idea you had isn't your only option for bringing in revenue. In the grand scheme of things, once you find the right business concept, you can make more.

Jim Cocks gets this completely. He's had multiple careers over his life. He started as a singer and dancer until an injury forced him to transition into business. Even then, he had several false starts before he found his success with Level Up. As he told me, "There's no such thing as overnight success. Before Level Up became a million-dollar business, I had three or four businesses that didn't make it. I tried everything from a supplement brand to a life coaching service, even an art store for local creatives." What I love about Jim's perspective is that he sees each failed attempt as a stepping stone to the next opportunity, not as a personal failure.

Now, Jim's advice isn't to give up as soon as things get difficult, or to throw in the towel just because growth takes longer than you expected. Pia Silva's experience with No BS Agency is a perfect example of this. When she started the business, she was hoping it would give her a flexible lifestyle quickly. As she told me, "We eventually got there, but it took a lot longer than I thought and I had to learn a whole bunch of things I didn't know I didn't know." She thought she'd be able to work from anywhere within a couple of months or years, but it really took significant learning and some major mindset shifts before her business reached that point.

The key is that she did get there eventually, and she wouldn't have if she'd given up too soon. If you're making consistent progress, even if it's slow, then it's often worth it to stay the course. When a product, service, coaching program, or entire business has just become a money pit and is yielding no results, especially if it's also causing you stress or interfering with other aspects of your life, that's when it's time to take a hard look at whether it's time to let it go.

There's another common entrepreneurial mistake hiding in Pia's experience, and it's one I see all the time: acting on assumptions rather than verified facts. This could mean making assumptions about entrepreneurship in general, or about more specific things, like assuming you know what customers want instead of actually asking them. Nick Rodsater made this exact mistake when he was starting his chiropractic practice. As he explained to me, "I was so passionate about chiropractic care and health that I just assumed that everyone was, and that we would open our doors and be flooded with people who thought exactly the same as us." The reality? Most people don't prioritize their health until they're already in bad shape. This meant Nick had to completely shift his approach to getting his message out and helping people understand the value of what he offered.

People are always selling the thing they think their customer wants, but there's often a big disconnect between what they think people want and what people actually want. I've learned there are basically three stages people go through: they don't know they have a problem, they know they have a problem, or they know they have a problem and are looking for solutions. Too many entrepreneurs get stuck trying to sell to people who don't even realize they have a problem yet. If your target audience doesn't even know they have a problem, it's going to be an uphill battle to convince them to spend money on your solution. Entrepreneurs today have access to so much more data and information than we used to have. Take advantage of this before you make any big moves to verify not just that there's actually a market for your product or service, but also where your potential customers are in their thinking process. There will likely still be times you need to trust your gut, but having more information leads to better decisions and lowers the odds you'll need to completely change course because things didn't turn out as you expected.

I've already talked about a lot of mistakes, both here and in earlier chapters, and there will be even more coming as we move through the book. Obviously, you want to avoid making the ones you can, but I'll reiterate what I said to start the chapter, because it's important to remember: realistically, you're not going to avoid all of them. Making mistakes is an inevitable part of being an entrepreneur, or, really, of being human. When you do make a mistake, even if it's one you've already made before, don't waste energy beating yourself up. You only make it worse if you let it paralyze you or steal your momentum. There's a saying my kids grew up hearing in sports: Next play. In other words, if you missed a shot or threw a bad pass, don't dwell on it. That mistake has already been made, and you can't change it now. What you can control is making the best possible moves on the next play. Keep your focus on the present and future.

As an entrepreneur, this means focusing your energy on learning what you can from the mistakes you make and applying that knowledge to do things better. Analyze the situation to identify what went wrong and what you could do differently next time to change the outcome. I can tell you from experience that I've learned much more from the mistakes I've made than from my successes. When I think about it, this is actually true both in parenting and in business. Treating mistakes as learning opportunities can also help you get over that "sunk cost" mindset. Don't think of the time and money you invested as wasted, but instead as the cost of learning those lessons. Gaining as much wisdom as you can from each misstep is how you make the most of that investment, and can hopefully help you spot more of the pitfalls in the path ahead.

Key Takeaways:

- **Mistakes are part of the gig**: It's not if, but when. How you handle them is what counts.

- **One-size-fits-all advice is BS**: What works for Joe Schmo might be a total fail for you. Trust your gut.

- **Know when to fold 'em**: Don't throw good money (or time) after bad. If it's not working, cut your losses and pivot.

- **Screw-ups are learning opportunities in disguise**: Mine those mistakes for all the wisdom you can. Then do better next time.

The School Age Phase: Business Puberty (And Other Awkward Growth Stages)

Sending your kids off to kindergarten is huge. For the first time, they're doing things on their own: making friends, picking their own clothes, joining activities. They're developing independence and building fundamental skills, but they still need structure and guidance. They're not ready to tackle everything alone yet, even when they insist they are.

Same with a business at this stage. It's starting to develop its own identity separate from you, but you can't go hands-off yet. It's still evolving and needs you at the helm. And just like with startups, there are common mistakes business owners make here. Some try to rush growth and scale before they have systems in place—the classic "we'll figure it out as we go!" approach. Others cling to systems that worked at the start, not recognizing that the business has outgrown them.

There's a saying: as a mother, you're only as happy as your unhappiest child. As a parent entrepreneur, sometimes that unhappy child is your business. I've found this happens most when RSG is about to enter a growth phase and needs more of my and Josh's attention. Your business will still need as much time as you put in during startup, just focused on different things: ramping up marketing and sales, strategically planning your next growth moves.

This section is about getting through that messy middle stage. We'll cover refining your business concept, building sustainable systems, managing money, and fitting the demands of a growing business into the rest of your life. This stage is chaotic: opportunity overload, system breakdowns, a stretched-thin team (especially if that team is just you). But once you get through it, you'll have a business ready to scale to its full potential.

CHAPTER 9

Prune for Growth and Dial-In with Data

A business is not a static entity. This is exactly why I love thinking about entrepreneurship like nurturing a child—because, just like kids, businesses grow and change over time. As a child grows up, their identity evolves. The same is true of businesses. Even if you did your due diligence to clarify your concept and identify your market, those things won't necessarily be set in stone forever. You might uncover new markets, come up with a great idea for a new product or service, or encounter an unexpected roadblock that forces you to pivot. Just think about all of those alcohol producers that started making hand sanitizer during the pandemic. I guarantee you none of them had that in their 5-year business plan, but the market changed, and they found ways to adapt.

Like many entrepreneurs, I have my own Covid pivot story. Pre-2020, attending trade shows was our main strategy for attracting new clients and growing RSG Sales. We'd do eight trade shows a year, of roughly 4–5 days each, which would add up to over a month away from my family every year. Not ideal, by any means, but a sacrifice I thought I had to make because it was our proven growth strategy. Granted, it was also the only strategy we'd ever tried, but it consistently worked, so why change it?

Then COVID happened, and everything stopped. If we wanted to keep growing RSG Sales through the shutdown, we needed to find another way to do it. I had resisted making videos for years, with the excuse that it wasn't our model, and trade shows worked fine. Now that those shows weren't an option, I sat down and made a 90-second YouTube video called "How to Sell to Wayfair" out of desperation. The video quality was terrible, but it turned out that didn't matter. That video ended up getting over a million views and completely transforming our business. It was only then that I realized that I had been making a classic entrepreneurial mistake: stubbornly clinging to what had worked in the past even though my business and family had outgrown it.

I know I'm far from the only entrepreneur to make this mistake. Many probably made it the same way that I did: without even realizing it was a mistake until something forced a change. A lot of times, when you find something that works for your business, it absolutely does make sense to keep repeating that process over and over. Changing too often and chasing every trend can be just as damaging for a business as clinging to processes, people, or products and services that you've outgrown. It isn't easy to identify when it's the right time to try something new. One point when it's often smart to step back and assess is when you're no longer a brand-new startup and ready to start thinking about growth. Part of making this transition smoothly is taking a close look at your business concept and refining it to match your current reality and what you see coming in your future.

In the early days of a new business, it's common to just throw a bunch of things at the wall and see what sticks. This can take a lot of forms. For product sellers, it can mean creating lots of designs and items across various categories to test which ones appeal most to your audience. For service businesses, it could mean offering a range of different adjacent services (power washing and deck sealing and driveway repair, and...), or being open to a wide variety of clients. When we first started RSG Sales, we weren't picky about who we worked with. Our main screening requirement was "Can they pay?" If the answer was yes, then we'd work with them. We were still approaching things with a scarcity mindset and the back-of-the-mind fear that, if we turned a potential client away, there might not be another one knocking on our door to replace them.

I won't say that open-to-all mindset was a mistake. It probably did help us to grow faster when we were building our brand, but it also led to some aggravation from taking on clients who weren't a good fit for us. Now that we're established, we're much more specific about what type of client we want to work with and have no problem saying no or firing clients who don't align with that vision.

Robert Patin learned a similar lesson about client fit a couple of years into his business. He's always had a passion for working with creative business owners, but when he first launched his company, he did it as a generalist. This let him quickly build a full roster of clients. The problem was, he didn't necessarily enjoy working with all of them. "I was being pulled in so many different directions with their business nuances and software nuances and things like that," he says, which quickly stole the passion that had made him want to start the business in the first place. His solution? "I decided to go back to where I wanted to be and ended up firing a lot of business about two years in." In hindsight, he realized that if he'd specialized in creative businesses from the start, he would've enjoyed running his business a lot more from the beginning.

For a new business, it can make sense to chase a lot of different opportunities. You're still homing in on your business identity, and often the best way to do that is to try a few approaches to see which ones succeed and which ones don't. That isn't sustainable once you reach the growth phase, though. It might sound backwards at first, but in many cases, the first step to achieving sustainable growth is to cut back, simplify, and refine what you offer. You can think of it like pruning a tree. When you remove damaged or diseased branches, it lets the tree focus its resources and energy on healthy limbs and promotes faster, stronger growth. The same thing happens when you prune a business by eliminating products, services, or portions of your customer base that don't drive much revenue or aren't aligned with your mission.

The million-dollar question, of course, is how to decide what you should prune out. In some cases, you can follow Robert's model and refine based on the kind of work that you enjoy doing. Identify which parts of your work excite you the most and which things you consistently dread, then look for ways you can prune away those dread-drivers and leave yourself more time and energy for the work that fuels your passion.

Another approach that works really well is the good old 80/20 rule, where 80% of your results come from 20% of your effort. This applies to businesses, too. Review your sales activity to identify which products or services are generating the majority of your revenue. These are the areas where you're likely to see the most growth if you devote more of your time and marketing investment to them. Cutting back in other areas might feel like you're at a plateau, or even taking a step backwards, but this feeling is deceptive. You're not shrinking your business. You're removing the dead weight so you can feed and water the parts that will grow sustainably year after year.

In some cases, refining your business concept may mean making a more substantial pivot than simply trimming out low-revenue product or service categories. For Pia Silva, her growth really took off when she switched to doing two-day intensives for brand building instead of running a more traditional branding agency model. This decision was based on aligning the business to her and her husband Steve's lifestyle as much as it was about growing revenue. As she says, "The decision to move to the intensives model is what gave us the space and freedom for Steve to get back to being an artist, which was always the intention, but was very hard to do in the old agency model. It also gave us the flexibility to travel a lot, which is something we wanted to do. And it was while we were traveling that we decided we had enough financial and time freedom to actually afford to have a child, so this whole model is even the reason that I had a kid, because I don't know that I would have if we had continued to stress."

There is another side to refining your business concept, as well, which Robert Patin alluded to: focusing on the right audience and customer base for how you want your business to grow. This is critically important when you're deciding where to invest the most for marketing. I've heard the same problems over and over again from entrepreneurs who watch their marketing budgets balloon while their client list barely grows. Often, the problem is that they're creating ads their target audience will never see because they're on the wrong platforms. Spending thousands on Instagram or Facebook ads won't produce many leads if your target audience is professionals in their 50s who primarily use LinkedIn. If you want to fuel growth, understanding who your target consumer is and where to connect with them is just as important as refining your business identity.

This is another mistake I've made personally. In the early days of E by Design, I spent nearly $10,000 on a trade show because I saw that all of my competitors would be there, which made it seem like a place I wanted to be. Unfortunately, it turned out those competitors were still going mostly out of habit, not strategy. Our ideal clients had stopped going to that show years ago, and I came home with zero leads and a very expensive lesson. After that debacle, I implemented a proper tracking system to measure cost-per-lead and cost-per-acquisition across all of our marketing channels. This allowed me to set a maximum customer acquisition cost based on the average lifetime value of our clients and, most importantly, gave me data about which activities didn't produce results, so we could stop spending money on them, even if it was uncomfortable to do so.

If those metrics I just mentioned sound like so much Greek to you, then it's time for you to get to know your numbers. Refining your business concept isn't just about clarifying your identity today, but also what you want it to become: if you plan to scale, and if so, how much and by when. And if you want to make that growth strategically instead of just hoping to do it through luck and pluck, you need to understand things like which marketing approaches drive the most conversions, how much you can afford to spend to get new customers, and how many leads you need to hit your growth targets.

Understanding your numbers also helps you to see the true costs of each product you make or the services that you provide for clients. Profit margins can sometimes be deceptive if they're not factoring in things like labor and other operational costs. To see your real profit margins, subtract your total top-line sales from your actual expenses (based on real data from invoices or receipts—not your guesses of what your expenses should be). One of the best ways to determine what your rates should be is to reverse engineer it from your goals. For example, if you want to make $250,000 in top-line sales, divide that number by the cost of your program. This tells you how many you'll need to sell to hit your goal. If that number isn't attainable, raise your rates until the total sales you need to make sound reasonable. If you don't have a total revenue goal in mind, you could also simply decide what you'd like your profit margin to be, calculate where you'd need to set your rates to achieve it, then compare it against competitors to determine whether the market will support those rates.

It's common for new entrepreneurs to undercharge, especially those who are in a client or service-based business, and most especially, this is common among female entrepreneurs. One of the steps you may want to take when refining your business concept is to re-evaluate your pricing to make sure it both factors in your true costs and reflects the real value you provide to your customers. This can be uncomfortable when you have existing clients who are used to paying your old price. On the plus side, if you're currently undercharging, raising rates can be another effective way to prune your customer base. People who care about quality and appreciate the value of what you offer will be willing to stick with you, and you can clear out the people who are only interested in getting the cheapest product or service they can (who are usually also less-than-ideal customers in other ways).

Ultimately, the takeaway from all of this is that shifting into the growth phase of your business isn't just about ramping up your marketing and expanding your team. Before you do that, take a close look at your concept and make sure you know where you want to grow. That way, you'll invest in productive marketing and hire the right people into the right roles, and you'll be less likely to throw money at things that don't move your business forward.

Key Takeaways:

- **Get laser-focused as you level up**: Zero in on your most profitable offerings and ideal clients. Trim the rest.

- **Prune your biz regularly**: Scaling sustainably means cutting what's not serving you anymore, even if it worked in the past.

- **Base targets on real talk, not wishful thinking**: Let data drive your financial projections and marketing spend. Gut feelings are great, but numbers don't lie.

CHAPTER 10

From "That's Crazy" to "That's Possible": The Mindset for What Comes Next

Here's a truth most entrepreneurs already know from first-hand experience: when you're first starting, there's going to be lots of trial-and-error. It doesn't matter how much you plan, or if you have tons of experience working in (or even leading) similar companies. This business is its own beast. Everything from its brand identity to its ideal customers and growth goals is unique, and that means the struggles and opportunities you encounter running it will be different, too. You can limit the "error" part of trial-and-error by making smart decisions that are based on facts and metrics instead of gut feelings, but you're probably still going to need to take some leaps of faith and experiment a bit to learn what works and what doesn't.

It's when you get out of the startup stage that you can start to really make more strategic decisions. That doesn't mean you'll stop trying new things, but you can draw from your lived experience to take more targeted risks, the ones most likely to pay off and lead to growth. This is another place where businesses are like kids. No amount of book learning can fully prepare you for actually raising a human, and you'll probably feel overwhelmed and make a lot of mistakes at first. But as you go, you learn your kid's habits, your family's routines, and what pieces of wisdom and advice actually apply (and which ones don't). You'll have to keep adjusting as your kid grows up, but you're on a more solid footing and can make more educated guesses about what to do next.

Now, making this mental shift to be more strategic doesn't necessarily mean planning out every single move you make. It's more about confirming that every step builds on your mission and moves you toward your long-term goals. Exactly what that planning process looks like depends on your business and personality. Jim Cocks taught me something important about this: "Everyone has a different style. Some write 300-page business plans and stick to them. That's not me. Business evolves fast, and while I always have goals and a quarterly focus, I also know things can change overnight. So I stay flexible, but intentional."

What I love about Jim's approach is that he knows exactly where he wants his business, community, and team to be in 12 months, but he leaves space for the unexpected. That doesn't mean he just wings it, though. His non-negotiables are the KPIs that give him an accurate picture of where his business is today and whether he's making consistent progress. As he put it to me, "Your team can't live inside your head. Set the numbers. Make sure everyone knows what success looks like. Then it's not about opinions. It's about execution."

This idea of leaving space for the unknown means you can keep trying new things, but following metrics means they're not random shots in the dark. You're choosing risks selectively, picking the ones that make the most sense for your vision and have the most potential to deliver a big return. When you spot that kind of opportunity, even if it's something big and scary, Jim's advice is something I'll never forget: "Say yes and work it out later. So many people hesitate because they're afraid of failure, of being unprepared, of the unknown. But most of the biggest wins in my life came because I said yes before I felt ready. Now, I'd add to that: it's okay to say no after you say yes if you realize it's not aligned. But don't close the door on opportunity just because it's uncomfortable. Say yes. Shit your pants. Grow."

I've seen this play out perfectly with Jade Green. She used to be terrified of public speaking; she literally would throw up in a plant before stepping up and hide from every opportunity. But the moment she finally embraced the stage and leaned into speaking instead of shrinking from it, that's when everything changed for her business.

Brittany Pickrem has learned the same lesson. As she told me, "Any time I do something completely scary, there's only good that comes from it." But she also taught me there are different types of fear to pay attention to. You need to ask yourself: is this fear because I'm actually in danger, or is this fear because I'm about to grow and do something totally different than I've done before? If it's the growth kind of fear, that's when you know you need to push beyond your comfort zone. Every time your business levels up, you'll be entering unfamiliar territory. Your systems, metrics, and vision are the anchor that keeps you grounded while the business soars to new heights.

What I also appreciate about Brittany's perspective is that she doesn't think growth opportunities need to be rushed. Slow growth is still growth, and steady progress is often more sustainable. As she put it, "Because of technology, we're focused so much on speed. I identify with a turtle. I do slow and steady. I want to make sure I feel the ground beneath my feet. It's okay to go slow, and it's okay to be small. It's okay to not feel adequate or enough. You are enough because you're here."

There's one detail in there I want to highlight because it's both important and easy to overlook. Notice that I said "your business' mission and identity," not *your* identity. You and your business are separate things. That might sound obvious, but for entrepreneurs it's often not. We pour our energy, passion, sweat, and tears into our businesses, especially early on. A lot of times, that means the boundary between the founder and the business gets very blurry.

Why is that a problem? Because you can't effectively lead something that you see as an extension of yourself.

So how can you tell if you still need more separation between you and the business? There are a few signs to look out for. For one, when criticisms of your business feel like personal attacks. On the other side, you might struggle to give feedback to employees or contractors because you feel like you're being mean. Another big sign is if you can't imagine the business running without you. That's often because you haven't created documented systems for everything, and some aspects of the business still exist only in your head. Or in some cases, even when you have systems in place, they don't feel real because you make exceptions to them based on how you feel that day.

The growth phase of your business is an excellent time to solidify your separation from it. This is mostly a mindset shift, though there are some small actions you can take to help. One is changing how you speak about the business and your work. Start referring to it in the third person.

Instead of asking "What do I want to do?" ask, "What would be best for my business?" Something I did (that might sound kind of woo-woo, but it worked) was to create a business entity in my head. I literally visualized RSG Sales as a separate entity that had its own personality and needs.

Putting boundaries between you and the business also helps to reinforce this separation. This starts with the basics like having a business bank account, so there's no confusion between your money and the company's money. Do the same thing with time by setting regular business hours if you don't have them already. When you're "off", you're just you, not the leader of your company.

These seem like small things, but I promise, once you make this shift, the difference will be night and day. You'll be able to make more objective decisions and more clearly evaluate what's best for the business, not what feels best for your ego. Criticism flows more easily in both directions because it's no longer personal. If an employee isn't performing, or a client isn't happy with their service, that's not a rejection of you; it's just not working for your company. It also pushes you to create actual systems and processes that can work without you instead of acting on instinct and memory. Once those are in place, you'll be better able to develop a strategic vision and guide the big-picture direction of your company's growth, something that's almost impossible to do when you're down in the day-to-day weeds.

Achieving this separation fully can also help you to push through some of the other common frustrations of entrepreneurs in the growth stage. One of the biggest ones is brain drain and decision fatigue. Just existing as a human means you need to make a lot of decisions over the course of a day. Being a parent or caretaker adds to the decision load, then being an entrepreneur piles even more on top of it. It's no wonder that parent entrepreneurs, especially, feel like their brains are batteries constantly getting drained and never charged.

Here's something I learned that might surprise you: decision fatigue is actually a real thing that scientists have studied. Turns out, every decision you make depletes your brain's energy levels. This is as true for small decisions like "What's for dinner?" as it is for massive decisions like "Should we take on this $100K client?" And when you've made too many decisions, your brain basically starts malfunctioning. The part that considers consequences and the part that controls impulses stop talking to each other properly. It's like your brain's Wi-Fi just dropped to one bar. You're still connected, but you're definitely not getting the best performance.

When your brain reaches this level of decision fatigue, a few things often happen. You're more likely to procrastinate other decisions because your brain isn't ready to deal with them. Another form this takes is analysis paralysis, best exemplified by the feeling of standing at your open fridge because the thought of choosing what to eat feels as complicated as a merger decision. Or you might go the other way and hastily make major decisions because you're too tired to think them through, like the time I approved a $3,000 ad for a trade show that wasn't even going to be in a publication for my customers, because my brain had reached the "whatever, just do it" phase of exhaustion.

Separating your identity from your business won't completely cure decision fatigue, but it helps because business decisions are no longer yours alone to make. The systems and policies you've put in place let you make some decisions instantly, while others can be outsourced to members of your team. I have a "Save the Brain" framework I put in place that helps prevent fatigue from the decisions I can't avoid. At home, I use a mix-and-match capsule wardrobe and a repeating dinner menu that minimizes everyday decisions. I also pass business-related decisions through two tests:

- The 2-Minute Rule: If it takes less than 2 minutes and won't cost more than $500, I make the decision immediately and move on.

- The Done-Undone Test: Before any decision, I ask, "Can this be undone easily?" If it's reversible, I make the call; if not, I give it more time and energy.

Another common frustration for parent entrepreneurs in the growth phase is what I call Mom Guilt: that feeling that you're always working but still failing at everything. This isn't just something that parents face, either. Anyone who's trying to balance their personal life with being an entrepreneur can probably relate to this vicious cycle. When you work harder to build the business, you feel guilty because you're neglecting the other areas of your life; when you spend more time with your kids, family, or friends, then business tasks pile up and the guilt with them. And, when you try to do both at the same time, you don't do either with your full energy, which means—you guessed it—more guilt. The worst part is, research shows that guilt impairs decision-making and reduces productivity. In other words, the more guilty you feel, the less effective you are in every area of your life.

If you've experienced this, you've probably also heard some old standard advice from friends and family: to delegate more, set better boundaries, focus on self-care, or lower your standards. People who say these things aren't wrong, but this advice is incomplete and fails to acknowledge the very real tensions that come up when you're building a business while also trying to raise a human.

I don't have an easy fix for this one because I don't think one exists. What helped me push through this feeling was having an honest conversation with Josh about how overwhelmed I felt. It wasn't easy, but it opened the door to real solutions, like implementing regular family meetings each Sunday to balance and align our priorities for the coming week. Another big breakthrough happened when I let myself redefine "enough" in both my business and motherhood. I had to realize success didn't mean never missing an event, having perfect systems, or always being available for everything my family or team needed. Instead, success comes from building a business that aligns with my family and is sustainable long-term. The guilt didn't magically vanish once I had that realization, but it definitely helped it feel more manageable.

I'll wrap up the chapter with some advice from Robert Patin that has really stuck with me. A colleague who used to be a psychologist gave him advice back in his early twenties that changed how he approaches everything. She told him, "The best thing that you can do in development is to be a better steward of yourself, and be curious about your response to everything." Whether you're pissed off, happy, angry, sad, nervous, or anxious, whatever that response is, you should engage with it with curiosity to understand why.

Taking the time to reflect on your stress points, your moments of joy, and all the other emotions that come up as you build your business can help you to better understand how your emotions impact your decisions and the way you engage with other people and yourself. The better you understand that, the more success you'll have in balancing your business with the rest of your life in a way that's sustainable long-term.

Key Takeaways:

- **Evolve your systems with your biz**: What worked at the start won't cut it as you grow. Keep those systems in tip-top shape.

- **Map out your core processes**: Get your sales, marketing, client care, and money management dialed in and documented.

- **Delegate, automate, repeat**: The less your day-to-day depends on you, the more your biz can grow. Systematize yourself out of the equation.

CHAPTER 11

Five Point Guards Don't Win Championships

Look under the hood of any successful business, and you'll see strong systems are the engine powering their momentum. By the time you're making consistent revenue, you've probably already developed at least some basic systems to track finances, collect client information, document processes, store information, bring in leads through marketing, and close deals with your sales processes.

The good news is, those key systems don't change as you grow. The bad news: the specific systems you developed as a start-up often aren't the same ones you use as your business grows. Especially for bootstrapping first-time entrepreneurs, it's likely that at least a few of your systems were thrown together haphazardly when you realized you needed them, then expanded piecemeal as you used them. These systems can function well enough when you're small, but they're going to be nearly impossible to scale, and they're likely not as effective as they could be if they were refined intentionally.

The biggest issue, though, is that many founders view these first systems as separate entities, which doesn't reflect the reality of running a business. Everything in a business is connected, and the same should be true of the systems you use to run it. Trying to run a business without integrated systems is like going on a cross-country road trip without directions. Sure, you might get where you're going eventually, but you'll waste a lot of time in the process and, at some point, you'll probably end up frustrated in the middle of nowhere, wondering where you went wrong.

I have another analogy for the sports fans: having systems that don't work together is like trying to win a championship with five point guards. Yes, they can all play basketball, but if you don't have a shooting guard to score, a center to protect the paint, and forwards to provide versatility, there's no way that team can compete at the highest level. To win consistently, a basketball team needs different positions working in perfect harmony. The same is true in a business. Each system plays a specific role, but they also need to work together as one unstoppable unit.

To give you an idea of what I mean, here's how our systems work together at RSG Sales:

- Marketing brings in leads (our Point Guard directing the offense)

- Sales closes deals (our Shooting Guard, scoring those clutch points)

- Client onboarding welcomes new business (our Forward, adaptable, and reliable)

- Management systems grow accounts (our Center, dominating the paint)

- Finance systems track it all (our Coach, keeping us focused on our goal)

When all these systems work in tandem, that's when RSG Sales runs at peak performance. We have our marketing systems spotting ideal opportunities for consistent lead generation. Well-developed sales processes translate to high conversion rates, while smooth onboarding ensures clients get an exceptional experience from the start, so they're more likely to stay on our roster long-term. Management systems keep track of all our accounts so that client experience doesn't drop off over time, which drives sustained growth since new leads are actually additional business, not just a replacement for clients we've lost. Then, finally, we have strong financial tracking that makes sure we're profitable.

So how do you build integrated systems that deliver this kind of consistent high performance? I'll start off by saying: it doesn't happen overnight. Our current systems grew out of years of continuous improvement, tweaking them to address issues we didn't anticipate, remove bottlenecks, and get rid of redundancies. You'll likely do the same as your business grows. Your systems aren't etched in stone. Like the business itself, they're best when they're flexible and can adapt to your growth.

Jim Cocks learned this same lesson with Level Up. At the start, using free software and basic tools helped them move quickly and keep costs low. Eventually, though, they reached the point that the business outgrew these starter systems, and that's when they invested in more complex tools. As Jim told me, "We've evolved. We've got streamlined SOPs, team communication processes, and our CRM platform does the heavy lifting, from client tracking to course delivery to automation. That's the stuff that makes scaling possible."

What I learned from Jim's experience is that it isn't always easy to know when it's the right time to make this switch. In his case, a sudden influx of new business gave his old systems a stress test, and they failed. He explained to me what happened. "A few years in, I landed a dream partnership that gave us 20–30 new clients in 2–3 weeks. Total flood. But our systems weren't ready. We didn't have the team or the backend capacity to support it, and the client experience took a hit. Results dropped. Frustration grew. We struggled to keep up. If I could do it again, I would've said, 'Yes, but give me four weeks to prepare.' That way we could've scaled with quality, not chaos."

Pia Silva went through something very similar. As she told me, "There were definitely moments in the first couple of years of the coaching business that we just didn't quite have the systems in place to support the number of people coming in. It wasn't that we couldn't handle it; it was just that we weren't able to support it at the level that we wanted. Having a bunch of people on board at once created a ton of headaches on the back end because there were issues we had to take care of personally. That meant we were all burnt out because we were putting out fires, as opposed to taking actions that were furthering our future growth."

What I admire about Pia's approach is that they eventually stopped, stepped back, and redid the first portion of their program. "It felt like a huge investment of time and money, but the purpose of it was to make it easier to onboard clients and get them to that first mark of success. Once we had that in place, then we could support fast growth much more easily."

Here's the pattern I've noticed from talking to entrepreneurs like Jim and Pia: a lot of us finally improve and integrate our systems after our old way of doing things doesn't work the way it used to. If this happens to you, don't feel bad; you're in good company. But there is a way to avoid hitting the breaking point, and that's to take the time to evaluate your systems before you start to grow.

Ask yourself: What are the biggest sources of stress and frustration in your typical work day? Trace those issues back to their roots. Could you change your process or develop an SOP to eliminate that problem, or at least make it less disruptive and annoying?

Another great question to ask: What are the things that only you can do as the founder? You want this list to be as short as possible before you focus on growth. Granted, there will probably always be things that are so critical you want to stay hands-on with them, but that shouldn't be the only option. Building a strong foundation of systems means your business will survive if something happens in your personal life and you need to take a step back, and it lets you roll with the punches if there's a recession or other external shift that requires you to pivot. Anything that currently lives only in your head, figure out a way to make that a teachable, repeatable, scalable system. Otherwise, you can end up in a situation where you're the business's biggest bottleneck.

Kid-raising wisdom can help here, too. You don't just hand a mop to a 5-year-old and tell them, "Go clean the kitchen." You start with simple tasks and gradually increase their responsibility as they grow. You can apply the same idea to business systems. At the start, you're using "Make Your Bed" systems: dead-simple processes equivalent to a child's first chores. In business terms, these are things like basic checklists for routine tasks, simple forms to capture essential information, and clear guidelines for core tasks that anyone can follow. As your team grows, you can move to "Clean Your Room" systems, things that are slightly more complex and involved, but don't yet cede full responsibility. This is when you build connected processes that flow together, implement simple decision trees, and create documentation that explains the why of your processes instead of just the what and how. Finally, you can graduate to "Manage the Yard" systems that enable complete ownership. These systems allow team members to manage entire functional areas, integrate quality checks into the process, and let the team handle variations or complex decisions without your input.

Getting to that last stage doesn't just support smoother growth. It also means you can actually step away without worrying there will be a hundred fires to put out when you come back. Once RSG Sales had those fully developed systems, I could finally take a beach vacation and not think about work once, for seven whole days. And, let me tell you, it felt as incredible as it sounds. It helped my team, too. Good systems naturally eliminate micromanagement because everyone has clarity about their expectations and knows how to make decisions. That means you can focus on results, not constant oversight, and still be confident you'll get consistent outcomes.

I can hear what some readers are thinking right now. Something along the lines of, "All of this sounds great, but how do I actually do it?" The answer to that, unfortunately, is: it depends on the business and the system. But let's zoom in on one system as an example to hopefully give you a bit more clarity. One area where systems are both hugely beneficial and often sorely lacking is marketing.

A lot of times, founders start off with what I call the "spaghetti at the wall" approach. They buy ads, post on social media, attend industry events, and do whatever else they can think of to get their name out there. Then, when one of those things actually works, they just keep doing that over and over.

This can be a good way to get started, but it's not going to serve you well long-term. I learned this lesson with RSG Sales when we'd hit on trade shows as our go-to lead generation strategy and didn't even consider other approaches until the pandemic took in-person events off the table. That was terrifying in the moment, but proved a blessing in disguise because it forced us to develop a real marketing system that was scalable, lower-effort, and could be monitored and automated to produce consistent results.

To build this system, I started by identifying our clients' biggest pain points, then creating content that provided specific solutions to them. I focused this content on searchable topics, which I plotted out into a content calendar, so posts went out on a consistent schedule. I also repurposed this content across platforms to broaden its reach (without me spending all of my time creating unique posts for every single site).

Valuable content will help to drive leads to your site, but it won't convert them on its own. For that, it needs to be paired with a user-friendly way for people to get your product or service, either a well-designed and functional online store or a simple booking process. For service or client-based businesses, also build in a structured way to qualify leads. Use your ideal customer profile as a template. Whatever traits define your perfect client, whether that's where they live, what industry they're in, their income level, or some other factor, screen and score leads based on those factors. This helps you focus your energy on the leads that are most likely to pay off.

Those steps above are how you build a lead pipeline. The next step is having a system to manage it. Create a system to follow up with interested leads, and automate it as much as you can. Finally, figure out how you'll track the effectiveness of your marketing. Track responses to your ads to figure out which ones generate not just the most leads, but the most high-quality leads that actually convert. Also, keep track of how much you spend on each of those leads and the average lifetime value of the clients you landed from each source. This helps you decide how to allocate your budget to maximize the return you see for it. Once these pieces are in place, it's just a matter of maintaining and refining your system as you go to keep it relevant to your business and the market as they evolve.

This kind of methodical, system-driven work might seem like the "unsexy" phase of a business, but I honestly think the opposite is true. This is the point when you start to reap the benefits of the hard work you've put in, transforming your business from a toddler that needs constant oversight to a self-reliant entity that won't collapse into chaos the second you turn your back.

Key Takeaways:

- **Your systems need to play nice**: Build processes that talk to each other, not operate in silos.

- **Level up your systems as you scale**: Investing in slicker tools and tighter processes pays dividends in the long run.

- **Prioritize high-impact work**: Don't confuse busy with productive. Focus your energy where it moves the needle most.

CHAPTER 12

Know Your Numbers (Even if Math Makes You Twitchy)

Every business, whether it's a multinational corporation or a one-person side-hustle run out of their living room, has one shared goal: to earn revenue. This might sound obvious, but there's a reason I'm reminding y'all. A lot of entrepreneurs don't run their business like they're trying to make a profit. You can sometimes get away with some bad financial habits as a brand-new startup, but those problems are going to really start biting you in the butt once you start to grow.

The single biggest money mistake that entrepreneurs make is not understanding their numbers. This isn't just about keeping your books accurately (though that's definitely something you want to do, too). The problem starts even further down for many people: they don't understand which numbers they should track to really get a handle on their financial health. This gets back to what I talked about in Chapter 4. Top-line revenue doesn't give you the complete picture on its own. What you really need to pay attention to is profitability; in other words, how much you make after all of your expenses are factored in.

And I do mean all expenses. Not just inventory and operational costs. Many entrepreneurs don't actually know where they're spending their money, even if they use accounting software, and often the root problem is that they don't review their accounts regularly to do a financial check-up. That's also what leads to people wasting money on unused subscriptions they forgot to cancel, or underestimating product costs because they don't realize their supplier raised their shipping prices. If you're paying attention to your money, you catch these kinds of things much faster. I like to physically enter expenses into a spreadsheet because it makes them tangible and forces me to look at and justify each one.

To do this kind of financial check-up, you can start by reviewing your bank and credit card statements. But you also need to factor in things that don't show up as recurring expenses, like taxes, yearly subscriptions, or returns and damaged inventory for product-based businesses. This is where it becomes super helpful to have multiple dedicated business accounts. I have one account for income that everything comes into. Then, I distribute it between my operating account (for day-to-day expenses), a payroll account, and an account I use for taxes and profit. This way, I know I always have money to not just take care of everyday expenses, but also cover my tax bill and pay my staff—and to pay myself, too.

Let's pause there for a second because a lot of entrepreneurs need to hear this: Yes, you should pay yourself. Nearly every entrepreneur's first instinct is not to pay themselves at first. The logic is that it's better to reinvest that money into the business and that they'll start taking a salary after they're making consistent revenue. In the very early stages of a new business, this might be necessary. Exactly how long it takes to make a business self-sustaining depends on a lot of factors, like your industry and whether you're growing it full-time or as a side-hustle.

Even very successful businesses often aren't profitable at first. Danielle Ratliff learned this with both of her businesses, which took a few months to start earning consistent revenue. As she told me, "If you expect to generate revenue right away, you're just going to upset yourself and be stressed the F out all the time." Her advice is to give yourself at least two years before you plan to generate enough revenue to support yourself and your family. In the interim, you want to have other money to draw from, whether that's your savings or a second source of income. Notice, though, that Danielle didn't say you won't bring in any income, just that you shouldn't expect to support yourself solely with your business right off the bat.

The biggest problem with not paying yourself at all, aside from its impact on your personal finances and mental health, is that it gives you an inaccurate sense of your business's costs. Your profit margins will be inflated if they're calculated based on you providing free labor. By extension, everything else you base on these profit margins, like your pricing or your long-term revenue goals, will also be skewed. This will eventually lead to a rude awakening when you decide to hire a team and suddenly find your costs skyrocketing.

Not paying yourself is also a ready-made recipe for burnout. It takes a ton of work and energy to build a business, and if you're not getting anything back for that effort, that's going to start building resentment—especially if you already have team members who are making more than you are for putting in a fraction of the work.

I've seen this play out painfully with entrepreneurs like Pia Silva. As she shared with me, "I learned the hard way about profitability. I was just concentrating on top-line revenue, but I didn't value our time. I just tried to make enough money to survive. And that worked pretty quickly, but we did find ourselves working all the time. My solution to working all the time was to hire employees. I then increased our prices to cover our costs, but because I wasn't aware of how to calculate profitability, I ended up bringing in a lot of revenue but landing us in debt."

What Pia wishes she had understood from the start is something she teaches other people now: how to build a high-profit business. "If I wanted employees, I would only get them after I knew I was delivering in a profitable way."

Nick Rodsater hit a similar snag when he was growing his chiropractic practice. One major mistake they made when they started really growing their team was not knowing their profit margins the way they should have. As Nick explained to me, "We didn't know what it cost us to see patients and how adding new team members would influence that. By not knowing the numbers, we didn't adjust our fee schedules properly, and we set up bonus structures that paid team members more, even if they didn't do as much work. We, as the owners, did more work but didn't get the same kind of bonuses."

What I learned from both Pia and Nick is that you don't have to fall into the same trap. The way to avoid it? Start paying yourself as soon as you can (ideally from day 1) and factor your labor into your costs even if you're not moving that full amount into your personal account yet. This gets you into the habit of treating your own time as valuable and prevents you from overestimating your profitability because you're already in the habit of factoring payroll into expenses. As your revenue grows, increase your own pay until you're making at least the going market rate for an employee in your industry. Don't even think about hiring other people until you're able to do that consistently.

My next advice for money management in a growing business: even if you don't plan to hire an accountant or bookkeeper, you should at least talk to one and get their advice once your business is making consistent revenue. Pick someone who has experience in small business finances, ideally someone who has worked with businesses similar to yours. Books like this one are great for general advice, but here's the thing: I'm an expert in my business, not yours (and not the field of accounting). I can tell you what worked for me, but that might not be the best move for you. Accountants can also help you find the best way to manage your finances to save you money on your taxes, like deductions for businesses run out of your home, or whether an LLC or SCORP will make the most financial sense. They can also stop you from making expensive mistakes, like misclassifying employees or missing filing deadlines, that can hit you with needless penalties and fees.

Having a financial professional on your side will almost always save you more money than you spend, and is a must-have before you start striving for significant growth. It's an especially good idea if you plan to hire employees. Jade Green learned this lesson when she was preparing to grow her team. She worked with a fractional CFO to build a full cash flow plan that helped her figure out the right time to hire. As she told me, "I made sure I could bankroll at least four months of their salary and give them time to get up and running. It was all about using the numbers to make smart hiring decisions, and I 100% recommend others do the same."

With that said, I have a few more revenue management tips to share for entrepreneurs who want to grow their business. First, I'll say that underestimating expenses isn't the only common problem. Just about every entrepreneur, and actually, just about every salesperson, overestimates what they're going to sell. It's the nature of the sales mindset. You want to shoot for the stars. And having big goals can be great, as long as you're also staying grounded in reality. You don't want to base your financial projections on your best-case scenario. This is only going to set you up for stress and disappointment. Go ahead and have that "in a perfect world" goal, but also pick a lower number that is the amount you're happy to live with, and use that lower number as the basis of your financial planning.

How do you figure out your "happy to live with" number? Your expenses are a good place to start, or your "nut," in business terms, which is basically the amount you need to cover your expenses and nothing else. This is the absolute minimum that you need to bring in for your business to be self-sustaining. Odds are you want to shoot for a bit more than just breaking even, but establish that baseline first so you know your must-earn income. Once you've got this number in money terms, translate it into whatever you sell to figure out how many total sales you need to make that amount. This is where things will start to look very different depending on your business model. If your nut is $1,000 and you're selling $10 widgets, you'll need to sell 100 of them every month just to break even. On the other hand, someone selling a $1,000 coaching program only needs to sell one a month to cover expenses, and everything on top of that is profit.

The next step, once you've identified your nut and minimum sales to meet it, is to decide how much profit you want to make. The exact margin you shoot for will be different depending on the business. For most product businesses, a margin of 25–30% is considered good. It's usually higher for service-based businesses and lower for restaurants and food service (though there are obviously exceptions to every rule).

For the sake of easy math, let's say you want to cover your nut plus make a 50% profit margin. That means you'll need to bring in double your expenses. For that widget business, that increases your minimum sales to 200 a month. If that sounds doable, then you have your next financial goal. If it doesn't, then either you need to lower your profit expectations or you need to raise your prices. If you sell those widgets for $15 instead of $10, for example, then the number you'd need to sell to earn $2,000 in revenue a month drops from 200 to 134, which may be a more achievable goal.

Now, if you overshoot your baseline goal and actually hit your "shoot for the stars" number instead—great! That means you get extra profit that month. But don't expect yourself to achieve that higher revenue all the time just yet. Give it a couple of months to see if it's a one-time surge in sales or a sign of sustainable growth. I'd say you should wait until you're hitting that higher number consistently for six months before you raise your expectations and shift your old "best case scenario" number to be your new baseline.

There's one last aspect of financial management that we should talk about before this chapter wraps up, because it's both critical for growth and an area where lots of entrepreneurs make mistakes: understanding the ROI of marketing spend. A shocking percentage of business owners don't know what it costs them to bring in a new customer. This isn't just as simple as looking at the cost-per-click of the ads you buy. You need to put in the legwork to figure out exactly how much it costs for every customer you convert. That includes what you spent on all those clicks that didn't turn into customers and any campaigns that failed to attract leads.

The higher the lifetime value of a client, the more you can spend to attract them. At RSG Sales, we'll happily pay $5,000 to bring in a high-quality lead because our clients tend to have high longevity. We can expect to see upwards of $100,000 in revenue from a single client, which is an excellent return for spending a few thousand to attract them. But that math is going to be very different for a typical product-based business, unless you're in an industry like apparel, where it's common for customers to have high brand loyalty. This is another reason it's absolutely critical to understand where your revenue is coming from: it tells you how much you can reasonably afford to spend to attract new business. You can afford to spend more to attract customers when you have a recurring revenue model, whether that's through a high percentage of repeat business, a subscription service, or a business that often has recurring appointments, like house cleaning or a hair salon.

If you're paying more for marketing than you make in new business, then 99% of the time, that means you're doing something wrong with your advertising. There are some exceptions, like if you're launching a brand new service or product; in that case, it can be worthwhile to take a loss for a little while to build awareness and establish yourself in the market, with the expectation that it'll level out in the long run. Even so, though, you shouldn't be running at a loss for long. In e-commerce businesses, you can give yourself a runway of about three months from the launch. The timeline is shorter for service businesses. If you aren't getting conversions within six weeks, you probably need to take a close look at your offer.

There are ebbs and flows for your income in any business. Strong financial management prepares you to weather the dry spells and make the most of your extra income when sales are high. Getting the right financial systems into place early is one of the best things you can do to pave the way to consistent growth and scale your business to its full potential.

Key Takeaways:

- **Profit is queen, revenue is a handmaiden**: It's not just about what comes in, but what you keep. Mind those margins.

- **Pay yourself like an employee**: Be consistent, factor your salary into your operating costs, and raise your rates to make it real.

- **CAC is the new black**: Know how much it costs to land a customer and how much they're worth to you. That's the key to smart marketing.

CHAPTER 13

From Solo to Leader: The Awkward Truth

Y'all, let's talk about one of the awkward, sometimes painful things that almost every entrepreneur struggles with, and almost nobody talks about: the shift from being self-employed, in those early years when you are the business, to becoming an actual leader of a team.

I'll be real—this transition kicked my butt. And the thing was, I'd had leadership positions before. I was PTA president, committee chair, team mom, all of those "herding cats" style volunteer gigs. There are two big differences, though. For starters, the people I was leading in those situations were there by choice. The even bigger difference: nobody's paycheck depended on my decisions.

Leading a business team is a totally different ballgame. When I started hiring people, I felt completely out of my depth, and it showed. I made just about every mistake you can. I avoided tough conversations (hello, conflict avoidance), set inconsistent expectations, took everything personally, and experienced tons of decision paralysis.

And I know I'm not the only one who's had this problem. I learned this lesson from talking to Palak Shah, who told me the biggest mistake she's made with her business so far was not stepping into her role as a true leader early enough. As she explained to me, "I hired people and gave them flexibility, trust, and empathy, which earned me loyalty and love. But what it didn't earn me was high performance. I was still operating as a people pleaser instead of a CEO. I avoided hard conversations. I gave second, third, and fourth chances. I confused kindness with leadership."

What Palak finally realized changed everything for her business. "It wasn't until I started setting clear expectations, measuring outcomes, and holding people accountable that my business began to truly operate at a high level. I learned that leadership is not about control, but it is about clarity. Your team can still love you, but they need you to lead them."

Boy, do I wish I'd had Palak shouting that last part in my ear when I was first starting to lead, because that was a lesson it took me way too long to learn. Instead, I fell into a common trap: wanting to be friends with everybody on my team. I was one of those entrepreneurs who referred to my employees as "the RSG Sales family." In hindsight, that mindset was just about the dumbest one I could've had. I should've maintained more separation from the start.

Danielle Ratliff went through something similar with her team at Serenity Now. As she told me, "The struggle is when you try to become friends with everybody, and there are different personalities, it doesn't always work out. And when you're friends with everybody, when it's time to uplevel with the company, or there's a performance issue, it makes it really hard to have those conversations and have their respect at that point."

I've seen this pattern play out with Robert Patin, too, who's made the mistake of holding onto team members too long, out of loyalty or the hopes that they'll get better. Inevitably, this created animosity from his end, "which actually ended up kind of managing them out anyway, but managing them out in a less amicable split. I did this for a few years, not really recognizing how much damage it caused me, the business, and them."

What Robert learned from this experience is something every leader needs to hear: "Better, clear expectation setting and better management check-ins make for a better, more cohesive scenario, and end up with everybody in a happier place faster."

Jade Green's advice for when it's time to make a change really resonates with me. "If you're getting that icky, uneasy sense, it's time to have a conversation. Nip that shit in the bud. Most people leave it too long because they're avoiding the tough conversation. They don't want to confront it, don't want to pick the work back up themselves, so they drag it out. But that gut feeling? That's your cue."

You'll notice there's nothing in Jade's advice about making sure the employee is still your friend after this conversation. Because here's the thing that every business owner needs to drill into their heads: your employees don't need another friend, they need a leader. The whole "work family" concept sounds warm and fuzzy. It feels good to say, and it might even attract some kinds of employees. But when you treat your team like family, lines get crossed. Those blurry boundaries create confusion about expectations and accountability. Either you or your employees end up feeling taken advantage of (usually me, in my case, since my tendency to be kind was taken as permission to walk all over me and the rest of the team), and it's much harder to discipline or fire somebody that you see as part of your family. Trust me. I've done it, and it sucks.

There's definitely an allure to being seen as the "cool boss" that everybody loves. I fell into this trap because I wanted to be approachable and understanding. And those are good traits to have as a leader, don't get me wrong. The issue comes up when the leader prioritizes being liked over being respected. That's when you're more likely to make personnel decisions based on personal feelings instead of business needs, and when performance standards slip because enforcing the rules feels mean. I remember I once spent hours agonizing over how to address performance issues with an employee I'd gotten too close to. We'd shared personal struggles, celebrated birthdays together, and even gone on double dates with our spouses. After all that, how could I switch hats and tell her that her work wasn't up to par?

Here's the thing you need to realize: boss-employee friendships are always inherently unbalanced. You, as the boss, know (and set) the employee's salary and have the power to impact their livelihood. That instantly gives you more power in the relationship. It can also mean the friendship isn't equally voluntary for both parties. Some employees might feel obligated to socialize with you even if they don't really want to. I once had an employee who laughed at my jokes, agreed with my ideas, and always volunteered to help with extra projects. I thought this was a great friendship, until I learned the employee just felt pressured to be my "yes man" to protect their job. Talk about a gut punch.

Instead of hiring people you like and treating employees like your friends, an effective business leader treats their team as valued assets for the business. That might sound cold, but do you know what feels even colder? Sitting across from somebody who was part of your "work family" and seeing the betrayal in their eyes when you tell them it's not working out. You don't need to become some kind of emotionless BossBot. You can still be warm, kind, and supportive while maintaining clear professional boundaries. You do this by being approachable about work issues but not becoming a confidant for personal drama, and showing genuine care without crossing into therapist territory.

This starts with what you share and ask about in the workplace. It's fine to chat about each other's weekend plans or how your kids are doing in school, for instance, but you probably want to stop short of asking about their dating life or unloading about your marital struggles. Keep some kind of separation in place when you socialize as a work team outside the workplace, too. If you do a happy hour, make sure it has clear start and end times, and keep some limits on the conversation topics, like no divisive political arguments or no discussion of deeply personal issues.

Maybe the most important thing here, though, is consistency. The rules and standards of the workplace should apply equally to everyone, regardless of how much you personally like them. Everyone needs to be held to the same accountability measures and receive the same depth and type of professional feedback. When everybody is treated equally, there's less room for favoritism or confusion about roles. That clarity ultimately leads to a more respectful, positive, and professional work environment, where everyone is working together toward common business goals.

Learning how to be a true leader is one of the biggest hurdles entrepreneurs usually need to get over when they start growing a team. Another equally difficult thing to figure out is how many people you need to hire and when. Many small business owners hire too early and grow their teams too big, too soon.

Here's where Jade Green's advice really opened my eyes. "Build the business you want to lead, and then hire the people who let you lead that lifestyle. Before hiring, you need to look at your true strategy. Never bring someone on until you've mapped out your strategic plan. Know where you're heading over the next 3–5 years. Understand who's currently on your team, who holds accountability for each function, where the gaps are, and who your 'icebergs' are; the people silently sinking performance. Then, and only then, identify exactly who you need to hire to help achieve that vision."

What you can't do, Jade says: "Is just throw bodies at a problem and expect it to solve itself." She's seen the disastrous results of that approach first-hand. She recently worked with a business whose leaders thought headcount equaled progress. They grew their team and promoted people without proper direction. The result? They went from $6 million in profit a year to a $3 million loss.

Robert Patin learned a similar lesson on a smaller scale. At one point, he'd over-orchestrated the business and made it too complex, growing the team to 15 people. He's since cut that in half, and they're earning twice as much revenue with a 7-person team. Today, he approaches hiring decisions from a financial standpoint. As he told me, "I have to have the cash flow or reserves that allow me to maintain that person until they make a financial impact. I figure out what the financial impact this person should have and how long it is going to take, then make sure I can do it within that timeframe without any financial ramifications for the business."

The specifics of your business matter a lot here, too. Not every type of business needs the same size of team or should start hiring at the same point of growth. Pia Silva shared with me how she approached this: "I started to grow my team as soon as I had the funds; probably even before I had the funds, because I always knew that the business I was building required a team. I currently have four full-time people and seven part-time coaches. There are probably one or two additional people that we could have, but that won't be until I'm ready to really level up. For now, I just want to make sure that we're continuing to build our systems to strengthen the output of the current team."

What I learned from Palak Shah is to hire "when your vision outpaces your capacity. When you know what needs to be done, but your calendar is the bottleneck. That's your signal. I'm always evaluating based on two things: Is this team set up to deliver excellence at scale? And does it allow me to stay in my zone of genius? If the answer to either one is no, it's time to make a change."

The unfortunate truth is, knowing when to expand your team isn't always obvious, especially as a parent entrepreneur juggling a million responsibilities. The signs I look for that it's time to hire are similar to Palak's. The biggest one is if you're turning down new clients or projects even though you want to say yes. That means you've exceeded your capacity, and you need more hands on deck if you want to keep growing. Also, think about your performance as the leader. Are you making mistakes you usually wouldn't? Do you feel like you're spending all day on tasks that don't actually grow your business? These are red flags that your brain and schedule are at capacity.

Once you spot those signs, the question becomes who to hire. For that answer, start from the specific bottlenecks your business currently has. Track where you're spending your time for a week and make note of which tasks drain your energy the most. These are prime candidates for delegation, especially if they're tasks that don't align with your main strengths. Then, once you've pinpointed what kind of work your new hire will do, figure out roughly how many hours per week you'll need them and how much you're willing (and can afford) to pay.

The last detail to figure out is what kind of help to hire. We've used four types of help at RSG Sales, and each is ideal for a specific kind of work:

- **Interns**: Low-cost (or free) and eager to learn, but temporary and will require more training. They're perfect for seasonal work, clearing project backlogs, or as a way to hone your delegation skills, though they're not usually a good choice for client-facing roles (at least not right away).

- **Virtual Assistants**: Flexible and affordable, and don't need a physical office space. They're great for tasks that can be done any time and don't need direct oversight, like admin, basic customer service, social media scheduling, or email management. On the con side, they don't understand your business as deeply as an employee, and communication can be a challenge.

- **Freelancers and contractors**: Have specialized skills and allow you to scale the workload up or down quickly. While their hourly rates tend to be higher, that's balanced by the lack of benefit costs and extra flexibility (they only work when you have tasks for them). They're ideal for periodic needs or tackling specialized tasks, like ad management or graphic design. On the downside, they're not integrated into your culture and may even work with your competitors.

- **Employees**: Fully dedicated to your business, and can grow with you and get invested in your success. They're also the most expensive long-term option and require the biggest commitment. Employees are best for client-facing roles, long-term strategic positions, and core business functions that you don't want to trust to someone who doesn't understand your mission.

Those aren't either/or categories. A lot of businesses use a mix of permanent and contract-based talent. The type of help you hire for a given task might change over time, too. Maybe you start with a freelance social media manager, then evolve that into a full-time position as your business grows. You also don't need to go from 0 to 60 right away. Start small with 5–10 hours of help, someone who can handle a variety of tasks currently crowding your plate. College students are often excellent first hires. They need flexible work and real-world experience, making them perfect for intern-type positions.

Our team has gone through many different iterations over the years at RSG Sales. We started with interns and grew to a full in-house team of eight people. Then, three years ago, we realized it would be faster and cheaper to outsource some of those in-house roles, and decided to go leaner. We let go of our entire staff, rehired two different people, then filled in the rest of the gaps with contract labor that we can scale up or down as needed. This shift made RSG much more nimble and profitable. It's like Jade said earlier: headcount doesn't always equal progress. Sometimes, the best growth move isn't adding more, but restructuring what you already have to do more with it.

I won't sugarcoat it; building and managing a team brings a whole new set of challenges. But the freedom that comes from focusing on what you do best (while other people handle the rest) is absolutely priceless. The first summer we had an intern showed me what was possible when I stopped trying to do everything myself and allowed RSG to grow beyond what Josh and I could build on our own. Your business deserves that chance to grow past your personal capacity limits, and you deserve the permission to be the CEO instead of the do-everything employee.

Key Takeaways:

- **Up your leadership game as your team grows**: Ditch the friend hat for the boss hat. Set clear expectations and hold folks accountable.

- **Boundaries, boundaries, boundaries**: Friendly is fine; friends are trouble. Keep things profesh with your people.

- **Staff to your strategy, not your whims**: Let your long-term roadmap and financial projections guide your org chart. No gut-hiring.

- **Mix and match your squad**: Employees, contractors, or freelancers, build a talent cocktail that fits your needs and budget.

CHAPTER 14

Milestones, not Mayhem: Planning that Actually Works

It's the age-old question: Where does the time go? Most people say this as a hypothetical, but if you're an entrepreneur, you'd better darn well know the answer. If you don't, I guarantee you're leaving money on the table and making your life harder than it needs to be.

For anyone who feels like they're always working and still constantly crushed by a never-ending to-do list, I have a solution, but fair warning, you're probably not going to like it at first. The answer is time tracking.

I can already hear the immediate reaction of "Ugh, there's something else I have to do? I'm already drowning in tasks!"

I get this gut-level response. When the problem you have is too many tasks and not enough time, it's natural to have an instant "nope" reaction to what feels like just another administrative burden. Trust me, I've been there myself.

The irony here is that the time sinks you discover by tracking are probably eating up way more of your day than you'll spend actually tracking your time, even though it seems like just another task on the surface. And it's not just time that you'll save when you know how you spend it. Your revenue and margins will improve, too.

Let me explain that last bit. The truth is, money walks out the door when you don't track time. If you're like I was, you're probably undercharging for projects because you have no idea how long things actually take. That "one-hour client call"? It's really three hours once you add in the prep and follow-up. You think you'll spend two minutes answering emails or doing a "quick check" of social media? Once you start keeping track, you'll see that those small tasks can eat up hours of time across the week that you could be putting toward better things.

When I started tracking my time, I realized I was spending 90 minutes every day following up on tic-tac admin crap. Once I learned that, I outsourced those tasks to my EA (Executive Assistant), and suddenly I had time to actually grow my business. Because that's the thing: you don't just want to be busy. You want to spend your time on things that actually make your money. It blew my mind to realize I was spending more time on $10 tasks than on $1,000 opportunities. Once I knew that, I could flip the script.

Let me guess what's going through your mind right now about time tracking. You're picturing some complex system that you'll have to learn, with more reports and spreadsheets to manage, and constantly stopping your work to log it. Or maybe you're thinking about the apps and tools you've tried in the past, or previous failed attempts at tracking time. Some people have an emotional resistance to time tracking. Maybe you're a little afraid that you'll find out you're not as productive as you think you are, or anxious to learn how much time you've been wasting during your day. For people in creative fields, it can feel uncomfortable to put a ticking clock on that process, and sometimes it can conjure bad memories of working for bosses who look over your shoulder and give you that feeling that you're always being watched.

But here's the good news: tracking your own time doesn't need to be a complicated and prescriptive thing. My easy-peasy time tracking system doesn't use any apps or fancy tools; just a piece of paper with time broken down into 15-minute increments. As you go through your workday, mark down when you start and finish tasks. Do this every day for two weeks, then analyze your time use during that time. Divide your tasks into categories that make sense for your business. For me, these are things like email, client calls, team meetings, financials, marketing, short-term planning, long-term planning, and team management. You can add whatever other groups make sense for you. As I said, this isn't about fitting your work life into somebody else's model. It's about finding out how you're spending your average week.

Once you've sorted out your time into those categories, you'll be able to see exactly where you're spending your time. Fair warning: this can be a gut punch, but don't let it take the wind out of your sails. The whole point here is to find those places where you could be using time better. And the good news is, now that you know where your time sinks are, you can take real steps to reclaim that time for more useful things.

What you do next will depend on where you find out your time is going. If you're spending half your day on email, for instance, you could hire a VA to manage your inbox, designate specific email checking times, or create templates so it's faster to send common replies. If client calls are eating up all your time, the solution could be to put a maximum limit on call length, or block off specific days for calls so the rest of your week is open for other work.

All of this starts by asking yourself a few key questions: What's eating up most of your time? Where are you losing money? What keeps you up at night, and what opportunities are you missing? Once you have those answers in your mind, you can retool your schedule to use your time more intentionally. The time blocking advice I gave earlier in the book can be helpful here. That's how Jade Green wrangles her schedule. Every Sunday, she creates her ideal week. "I've put rules and boundaries in place so that when I'm focused, I'm 100% focused. That structure actually gives me the flexibility that I want. I'm intentional with how I plan my time. I look at what I want to do, how many hours I need, and who I need to staff up around me to make it happen. I refuse to get caught on the 'busy being busy' hamster wheel. Everything I do is reverse-engineered to build the life that I actually want."

That's a crucial thing to keep in mind for anyone who resists time tracking because it feels too constrictive. As Jade says, "Flexibility doesn't happen by accident. It comes from planning."

Having a team you can delegate tasks to makes this whole process so much easier. Pia Silva's goal is "to delegate anything and everything that I possibly can, which means I only handle things that only I can do. That has been my goal for years, and I'm getting closer and closer to it every month."

Here's something else I've learned: what works perfectly for someone else might be a complete disaster for your brain and your life. Your schedule should support what works for you, not force you into someone else's mold. Palak Shah has great advice to offer on this point. As she says, "One of the most important productivity strategies I've learned is to honor my energy rhythms. I don't force 5 a.m. routines or pretend I can pour from an empty cup. I work with intention, not hustle. And I always carve out space to think, because without clear thinking, I can't lead. I focus the energy where it moves the needle and aligns with my gifts. If it requires vision, trust, or high-level decision-making, I stay close to it. If it can be systematized, trained, or repeated, it gets delegated."

Now, before you can start sorting out which tasks deserve your time as the owner and which ones are less important, you need to know what's most important for your business. That means doing a bit of deeper planning to know where you are now, where you want to ultimately get to, and what milestones you want to hit along the way.

You can start small and build here, too. If you don't have any clear milestones in mind yet, start by setting some 30-day, 90-day, and 180-day objectives. How do you decide what those should be? Let me walk you through my strategy.

30-day objectives are going to be your "right now" priorities. These are your quick wins, fires that need to be put out, and opportunities that might slip away. Think about what things you have the resources to tackle right now and can complete in 30 days that will have an immediate impact on your business, or are costing you money or clients by not doing them. Some examples from my experience are things like creating templates for recurring tasks, setting up automations you've been putting off, or implementing a new team check-in or client onboarding process; things that will end up saving you time in the long run if you put a bit of thought into them now.

90-day objectives are things that require more planning and resources, but can be accomplished within a quarter. Usually, these will be things that need multiple steps to complete and will take more than a month to see results, but will still impact your operations. You don't want to create objectives just for the sake of doing it. That's just creating more busy work, which is exactly what you're trying to avoid. Examples of these are things like launching a new service offering, implementing a new project management system, developing a marketing campaign, or hiring and training a new team member.

The next level is the real game-changers: 180-day (or even 365-day) objectives. These are bigger strategic moves that will significantly impact your business's future. They take more thought and execution than the 90-day goals, but their payoff at the end will be bigger, too. You can identify these because they'll be things that require significant resources or investment, need extensive planning and coordination, and will impact multiple areas of your business or fundamentally change how you operate. Examples are things like major system overhauls, entering new markets, developing new product lines, or opening a new location.

One note here: before you move forward on these kinds of objectives, make sure you can truly afford to achieve them or to have them fail. Whatever the size of the objective you're setting, you don't want to bite off more than you can chew. I'd use a 3-2-1 rule on this one. Don't plan for more than three 30-day objectives, more than two 90-day objectives, or more than one 180/365-day objective at a time. This will help make sure your focus isn't getting split in too many directions and give you the best shot of actually achieving what you're building toward.

Here's another concept I want you to think about: setting milestones instead of goals, especially when you're targeting one of those bigger 180 or 365-day objectives. It's going to feel a lot more achievable if you break it down into smaller chunks and have mini arrival points you can celebrate along the way. You can take Jade's approach, but on a bigger scale. Instead of just mapping out the next week, think ahead to the next 6–12 months and map out targets to shoot for between where you're starting and the finish line. This lets you achieve degrees of progress that build toward a big achievement, instead of just having one massive "success or failure" goal (and feeling like a failure if you don't get there).

I like to think of milestones as stepping stones along a path toward where you want to be. That path might not be totally even, and some of the stones might be further apart than others, but you can still see exactly where you're going next without needing to look too far ahead or getting overwhelmed by the magnitude of what you want to achieve. When you take this approach, you can go after ambitious stretch goals without setting yourself up for a shame spiral. It's really about giving yourself the grace to love where you are right now and the permission to take small, actionable steps and make incremental progress.

Think about it this way. If you can accomplish 1% of a task in a day, that means you'll be 100% done in just over three months, and, if you keep putting in that amount of effort for a whole year, you'll be 365% ahead of where you are now. And, if you don't make the progress you were hoping for, it's much easier to figure out what went wrong and how to adjust so you can avoid that problem in the future when you're going step-by-step.

Growth doesn't always happen in a straight, orderly line, and it's very easy to get overwhelmed when you're in the middle stages of a business. Often, it comes in fits and spurts, and you might not realize you need more hands on deck until you're already drowning in tasks.

Growth in a child is the same way. One day, you wake up and swear they grew 5 inches overnight or are speaking full paragraphs. Business growth can feel just as sudden and surprising. By keeping track of how you spend your time and setting smart milestones to prioritize your work, you can push through the chaotic growth years without sacrificing your health or sanity in the process.

Key Takeaways:

- **Track your time to find the leaks**: I discovered I was spending 90 minutes daily on admin crap. Once I knew that, I outsourced it to my EA and suddenly had time to actually grow the business.

- **Set 30-60-90 day objectives**: Don't plan more than three things for 30 days, two for 90 days, or one big thing for 180 days. Focus beats spreading yourself thin.

- **Think milestones, not goals**: Break big objectives into stepping stones. 1% progress daily means you're 100% done in three months and 365% ahead in a year.

- **Know your numbers cold**: You can't manage what you don't measure. Track where your time actually goes, not where you think it goes.

CHAPTER 15

Work-Life Integration (because Balance is Bullshit)

Let's be real: building a business means putting in a lot of time. When you see entrepreneurs on social media talking about how they have so much freedom and flexibility because they're their own boss, they're not lying—but they're not giving you the whole truth, either.

With very few exceptions, they put in years of time, sweat, and money to reach that point where they could travel the world or be at every one of their kids' games.

Here's something else every entrepreneur needs to know: Work-life balance is a myth.

When I say that, I don't mean you should accept 80-hour weeks as the norm for the rest of your life. But when you're the boss, especially if your team is small or you're a team of one, it's often not realistic to expect you'll leave work behind every day at 5 p.m. That's more possible in some businesses than others, but for most of us, chasing that kind of work-life balance will only leave you frustrated and feeling like a failure.

At the same time, you can't push yourself to be constantly "on" for your business to the point that you ignore everything else in your life.

The traditional idea of work-life balance is designed for employees. In my experience, entrepreneurs are better off when they work toward work-life integration.

Jim Cocks puts it perfectly: "You're going to be 'on' for your business most of the time. That's the deal. Instead of trying to split your life 50/50, find moments where you can completely switch off."

Jim does this on two levels. Big picture, he goes overseas a couple of times a year. "Somewhere that my phone literally doesn't work. No contact, no stress, complete disconnection." He also finds micro moments throughout the day. "Step outside. Cuddle the dogs. Do something that shifts your energy. That keeps you fueled without needing a full week off."

Now, Jim runs an online business, which gives him flexibility by default. But this kind of integration works with brick-and-mortar businesses too. Nick Rodsater explains how he handles it with his chiropractic practice: "Being in a service business that requires hands-on work, our first goal is to have hours that give our patients access to us. But we've made strategic decisions about our schedule to give us time with family. We open multiple mornings a week so we can all start the day together, and we do half days on Fridays for family Friday afternoons. As we've grown and brought in new doctors, we can serve more patients while buying back some of our time to be with our family."

Life doesn't happen the same way week to week, and your business doesn't need to either. Palak Shah put this perfectly: "I don't believe in balance as a fixed state. It's a rhythm. Some seasons require more from the business, others from the family. The key is staying aligned and being willing to adjust when life calls for it."

There's no one answer for everybody. It's about figuring out a schedule that fits your business and your life. The ideal time to work toward this integration is when you're consistently earning revenue, but you're not aggressively scaling yet.

A lot of the things I've already talked about are going to help here. When RSG Sales first started, our annual Memorial Day beach trip wasn't a true vacation for Josh or me. We'd still work a few hours a day checking emails, jumping on quick calls, or putting out fires. That changed when we hired our first employee, and not just because we had help. What made the bigger difference was that we'd finally created systems that actually worked, including time-off-specific systems like notifying clients we'd be out of the office and establishing points of contact if they needed something before we got back.

Do we still have to handle unexpected problems during vacation sometimes? Sure. Nothing is perfect. But now we have peace of mind that we don't need to constantly check in. If something really needs our attention, our employees will reach out. If not, we can actually relax and push work out of our brains for a few days. That makes a world of difference in how refreshed we feel when we come back.

Integrating your work into the rest of your life isn't just about being able to take time off, though. Finding ways to keep yourself mentally balanced during your regular workweek can be even more difficult for busy parent entrepreneurs, but it's absolutely necessary to prevent burnout.

This gets back to what Jim said about finding things that shift your energy. You don't need to get away completely to feel refreshed. I'm going to tell you something that might make you roll your eyes at first: the best thing you can do is have what experts call a "third life"—something you do just for you, outside of your other commitments.

"But Heather," you're thinking, "how can I have a third life when I'm going crazy just finding time for my first two?"

I won't lie. It's not easy. Just like with time tracking and other "extras" we've talked about, though, once you carve out the space for it, the gains to your focus, energy, and overall mental health will help you make full use of the rest of your time.

If you're still not convinced, let me tell you about my yoga practice, or rather, what happened when I lost it.

Yoga was my thing before 2020. It wasn't just about the poses. It was where I found my center, my community, and my space away from business and family demands. Then COVID happened, and like everything else, yoga went virtual. I tried to keep doing it, but those Zoom classes just weren't the same. I'd lost that sense of community from being in the same room with other people, creating connections beyond work and home.

Turns out you really don't know what you've got 'til it's gone. That hit home for me after I lost my third life.

The entrepreneur's life can be a lonely one. Your days usually look like this: work your tail off building your business, rush home to handle family responsibilities, collapse into bed, repeat. There's not a ton of space in there for socializing. Having somewhere you can go and connect with people, not as a business owner or a parent but just as a fellow human, really takes the edge off that isolation.

This isn't just about mental health, either (though that's important too). Not having a third life can limit your perspectives, make you less resilient, and leave you more at risk of decision fatigue and energy depletion. Doing something just for you refills your emotional batteries—something entrepreneurs desperately need.

It doesn't have to be an active activity like yoga. Book clubs, church groups, anywhere you can find a community of people with a shared interest. But you need something to fill that gap. If you don't have anything right now, think about groups you used to be part of, friends you've lost touch with, or events you loved attending before the kids and business sucked up your free time.

The ideal is to pick something completely separate from your business. Don't treat it like networking by another name. Create a space that's pure fun, something based on your joy.

"Where do I find the time, though?"

Start slow. I'm one of those people who doesn't do things halfway. If I'm in, I'm ALL in. When I went back to yoga, I was tempted to jump right back to five classes a week. But I've been through that cycle before, where I sign up for everything, then flame out and quit a month later.

The trick with a third life is that it should give you more energy than it drains. If it doesn't, it's not the right activity for you right now. Do a test first. Sign up for one thing, once a week, then pay attention to how you feel, not just during it, but in the hours afterwards. That's your real energy ROI.

When I went back to yoga, I was tempted to try an evening class, thinking it would fit my schedule better. The problem is, I was already worn out at the end of the day, and working out would have left me feeling even more drained. So I started doing a morning class, and that was the sweet spot. When I leave now, I'm energized and ready to tackle the day. That's the feeling you're looking for.

You can always add more activities later, but it's hard to recover from burnout if you push yourself too much. Do the one activity for a couple of weeks, maybe trying it at different times to see which one leaves you feeling the best after. If you're eager for more, add one more session (just two activities total) and test that out.

Here's the kicker: make this activity something that is for real, 100% just for you. When I first decided to get back to my third life, I caught myself thinking, "I'll play pickleball because I can do it with Josh, so it'll count as a date," or "I should do an art class with my daughter." The problem? Those things would count as "family life", not a "third life." This is about having one thing where you're not wearing any of your other hats. Don't try to multitask it into something productive. Just let it bring you joy for joy's sake.

Giving yourself permission to have a third life can help with work-life integration, but it's not going to resolve another common issue for parent entrepreneurs: the sheer chaos that pops up when you're trying to wrangle kids, keep a house, run a business, and take care of your own needs all at the same time.

I remember one Monday morning that finally broke me. I was trying to get three kids off to school. Child #1 was driving and needed to be there early, and was letting everyone know it every five minutes. Child #2 was mad at Child #3 for some reason only they understood, and Child #3 was yelling back. This was the background while I was realizing Josh ate the leftovers that were supposed to be the kids' lunches, all while stressing out about the 8 a.m. meeting I still needed to prep for (and wondering why the hell I scheduled an 8 a.m. on a MONDAY), and realizing that two kids had practice at the same time that night in two different places and I had nothing to make for dinner.

It wasn't the best start to the week, to put it mildly. But in the midst of that chaos, I had an epiphany. This Monday's stress wasn't really about Monday at all. It was about what happened, or didn't happen, on Sunday.

That's when I started what I now call my **Sunday Reset**, and it changed everything.

It starts with a meal planning reality check. I plan dinner for the next week, making a note of which nights will need quick meals because of activities and other time crunches, then make a grocery list that actually matches that plan. I also use Alexa throughout the week to add anything I run out of to the list.

Next, I do a calendar debrief. This is a quick 10-minute look at what's coming up. I check for any double-bookings so I can fix them before they turn into emergencies, and make sure I've planned buffer time for the unexpected. I also note any early morning meetings that will require real clothes instead of yoga pants. I look at my work schedule, pick the three big things I want to accomplish this week, and write them in my calendar.

Lastly, I do a home reset. I spend about 15 minutes tidying up the main spaces and washing any laundry that absolutely must be done. Then I clear off the kitchen table drop zone (or wherever you stash mail and other things you're not ready to deal with quite yet) and pack any bags that are needed for Monday.

That's it. Three simple steps that help your next week get off to the best possible start. This doesn't have to happen on Sunday. Whatever day you consider to be your "weekend," set aside an hour at a time that actually works for your life. For me, it's usually around 3 p.m., and I set a timer so it doesn't turn into an all-day project. You can bring the family into it, too. Have the kids clean up their own clutter, or pack their own bags and lunches for Monday if they're old enough.

These activities are pretty tailored to my life, and that's the point. Whatever your biggest Monday morning stress points are, figure out ways you can solve them (or at least prepare to face them) on Sunday. I promise you, it'll save you hours of stress and chaos throughout the week. That right there might clear up the space you need to resurrect your third life.

It's not about completely changing your schedule or adopting complicated systems. It's about streamlining and being smart with how you use your time and energy so you don't have to choose between family, work, and fun. You can do all three.

Key Takeaways:

- **Work-life balance is a myth**: Stop chasing 50/50. Work toward integration. Find moments to completely switch off instead of perfect daily splits.

- **Get a third life**: One thing just for you, separate from business and family. Not networking disguised as fun. Actual joy that refills your batteries.

- **Sunday Reset saves the week**: One hour on Sunday (meal planning, calendar review, home reset) prevents Monday morning chaos and saves hours of weekly stress.

- **Start small**: One activity, once a week. Test when it energizes you versus drains you. My morning yoga works; evening classes leave me exhausted.

CHAPTER 16

Avoiding the Bright-and-Shiny When Your Business Gets Boring

The startup phase of a business is stressful, but it's also exciting. Everything you do feels new, with a whole slew of things to learn and seemingly infinite potential to grow. It's just like with a newborn: the business's whole life is ahead of it, so even when you're taking client calls on weekends or putting in another 10-hour day, it's easier to stay optimistic and focused on the future.

Eventually, though, that novelty wears off, and that's when the boredom sets in.

Now, I don't mean boredom in the sense of having nothing to do. I know some of you probably laughed out loud at the word "boredom" because you're thinking, "How could I possibly be bored when I have a non-stop to-do list constantly demanding my attention?"

You have to admit, there's a difference between being busy and being engaged. The type of boredom I'm talking about is more about how you feel and whether the things you're doing interest and excite you. So yes, you absolutely can be drowning in tasks and still feel bored with your business. In those awkward middle growth years, this is a problem that a lot of entrepreneurs have.

You've reached the point that things aren't new anymore, and hopefully, you have enough systems in place that your core operations are standard and routine. At the same time, you're probably not quite ready to take big steps to grow yet, and are more in the place where your best move is to keep making steady progress toward your current milestones.

This is an important stage in any business, but it's not the most exciting place to be. Because of that, this is when a lot of entrepreneurs are most at risk of getting distracted by what I call the "bright and shiny." That can take a lot of different forms. Maybe you suddenly get the urge to launch a new product or service, open a new location, invest in a fancy tech stack you don't really need, or even start a whole new business off to the side of your current one. Because when you already have ten plates spinning in the air, how much harder could it be to take it to eleven?

If you're looking for an example, Nick Rodsater made this mistake with his chiropractic practice in 2019. His first location was going strong, so he decided to open a second one, thinking that would boost their revenue and reach. Instead, he says, "In reality, it turned out to pull our focus and attention away from our main practice and lead to a lot of stress and frustration that slowed our overall growth rate at the main office. We learned a lot through that experience, but didn't see the business grow as expected."

Pia Silva's bright-and-shiny was a new coaching program she tried to launch in 2017, geared toward small service businesses. She'd just gotten pregnant and had the vision that she'd make the program profitable enough before she gave birth that she wouldn't need to do agency work during her new baby's first year. "Of course, that's not what happened," she says. "At seven months pregnant, I decided to abandon ship because I realized I was never going to get it where it needed to be quickly, and I really needed to get the stress off my head of trying to implement something that might not work and then have a newborn. It ended up being a good decision to shut it down, but it felt like a backwards step for me and like I had wasted all of that time trying to launch a business that I ultimately gave up on."

All that work wasn't wasted in the end. Four years later, she pulled from that experience and was able to get her No BS Agency Mastery Program off the ground quickly because of what she'd learned. But trying to start something new too early and too fast kept it from succeeding the first time.

The point is, this is the stage of growth where boredom is actually a good thing. It's when you can start to see all those seeds you've been planting bear fruit in the form of consistent revenue, repeatable processes, and steady, predictable growth. Those might not be the sexiest parts of business, but for me, they're exciting in their own right. It's like when your kid reaches grade school age. The routine you settle into during the school year might seem boring in the moment, but that boredom is actually a sign of success.

One reason that I think some entrepreneurs are susceptible to this kind of distraction is that they've made a different mistake: falling into the comparison trap. You know that feeling when you're scrolling Instagram and see another mom entrepreneur running a thriving business out of her impeccably organized office with her apparently well-adjusted children running around in the background? The one who launches new product lines while making homemade Halloween costumes without ever missing a soccer game? Don't you just hate that person!

The pit in your stomach is universal, and it hits parent entrepreneurs especially hard. We're comparing our businesses and our parenting simultaneously, with a side of home management and self-care thrown in for good measure. That's a lot of ways to potentially feel less than, and it's natural that it might send you scrambling for ways to do even more.

I haven't been immune to this either. Let me tell you about my million-dollar comparison mistake.

E by Design was a couple of years old and was doing a couple of million in sales, ranked as a top 5 pillow supplier on Wayfair. We were cruising. I'd built an amazing e-commerce business, but I thought I needed to build a brick-and-mortar to be fully legit. I was embarrassed to be "just" an online seller. Ridiculous, right? But that's how comparison warps your thinking.

Instead of focusing on the internet accounts that were running quite well, I had the "brilliant" idea to hire sales reps and get a showroom to attract interior designers.

This was just about the dumbest idea I could have come up with. Absolutely everything was wrong with this plan. We didn't have a program to sell to retail shops or designers. We didn't have the right infrastructure. We didn't have the right margins. We didn't have the necessary marketing materials. It was just plain old insecurity. I was too busy looking at the bright and shiny lifestyle companies that were really starting to take off, and felt like E by Design was "less than" in comparison.

I was so busy chasing somebody else's business model that I didn't even acknowledge how those companies probably would've killed to have my online sales. They'd all started in the retail store and interior designer space, and were trying to figure out how to sell online! I had it so backward.

Eventually, I came to my senses. After months of pointless work and tens of thousands of dollars, I could've invested in better things. The reality of the numbers should have shown me E by Design was an amazing online brand, one I should've been proud of instead of twisting myself in knots trying to keep up with the Joneses.

This is just one form of comparison trap that can derail entrepreneurs. You might see someone else's business model and think it looks better from the outside, making you question your entire approach. Or maybe you see other businesses growing faster, hitting milestones sooner, or getting more attention, without considering that different business models have different growth curves, or that "overnight success" usually has an invisible foundation built through years of work. Then there are lifestyle comparisons, where you're weighing the perfectly curated work-life balance someone seems to have online to your messy, chaotic Monday morning reality.

It doesn't matter which trap you fall into. They can all lead to decision paralysis because you stop trusting your instincts, lose authenticity from trying to force your business into a model that doesn't fit, and drain your joy and energy because you feel inadequate.

I took three steps to pull myself out of this trap. First: a reality check. I forced myself to look at the actual numbers instead of going on gut feelings. Data doesn't lie, and E by Design's numbers said our online sales were phenomenal, our profit margins were healthy, and our customers were happy. That's a success story by anyone's definition. I also started documenting our business wins to build an evidence bank against my "not enough" narrative. Finally, I started curating my influences. I unfollowed accounts that triggered comparison and sought out communities focused on collaboration over competition.

Avoiding comparisons can also help you reel in the common feeling among entrepreneurs that you always need to be doing more, that you need more courses to grow your knowledge, or more products to diversify income streams, or more hours and work to achieve the success you're striving for. That constant push toward more is one of the biggest mistakes I see business owners make.

Something it took me years to learn is that more often leads to less. When you have too many commitments, you can't focus fully on any of them. This can land you in the overwhelm trap, where you feel scattered, exhausted, and like you're drowning in work. And guilty on top of it because you realize you've taken on too much.

One insidious thing about the overwhelm trap is that it often creeps up on you so gradually that you don't notice until it's too late. You say yes to every opportunity because you're afraid of missing out, or take on "just one more" client or project, not realizing that will push your full plate toward overload. It's not until you find yourself completely paralyzed by your monster to-do list that you realize you're in trouble.

If you never feel caught up despite working regular evenings and weekends, especially if you also find yourself fantasizing about quitting or can't remember the last time you felt excited about your work, then it's likely you've fallen into this trap.

When you hit this point, the first thing you should do is pause and give yourself permission not to work on your business for 24–48 hours. Once you're more refreshed both mentally and physically, sit down and write out everything you need to do, then sort it into three categories: must do (contractual obligations and revenue-generating activities), should do (things that are important for growth but not urgent), and could do (things that are interesting but not essential). From there, you can choose one primary thing to focus on. You can still work on other things, but that primary focus target is your first priority. Block time for it into your calendar, then add in other "must-do" commitments around it. Do this until you've tamed your to-do list and feel back in control.

Having a support team can help get out of the overwhelm trap. Looking back on her time owning her massage business, Serenity Now, Danielle

Ratliff thinks outsourcing more could have helped her avoid the burnout that led her to sell that business. As she says, "My problem was I was trying to do all of it. I was massaging, answering phones, doing all the marketing and networking, and managing a team of fifteen people." The result was that she worked 80 hours a week and ended up so burned out that she had to step away.

I'll caution here, though, that this doesn't necessarily mean the answer to being overwhelmed is hiring more employees. I've mentioned it before, but it bears repeating: most entrepreneurs over-invest in their team early on, especially in service-based businesses. Pia Silva tried to hire her way out of overwhelm with her agency in 2014. In hindsight, she says, "I ended up in that situation because I had worked my butt off to bring in business and ended up having way too much work. I incorrectly thought the way to solve that was to hire employees. I wasn't profitable enough to support employees, but I didn't understand that at the time." She realized that problem when they ended up in debt despite bringing in a six-figure revenue. "How I solved that problem was I got rid of the employees, changed my business model, and turned it into something very high profit. We were out of debt within a couple of months, and we were making tons of money by the end of the year."

The bottom line here is that, if you're feeling overwhelmed, you can't just hire your way out of it. Instead, you need to identify how your schedule got too full in the first place, then fix that problem and center your focus on the work that really matters.

Honestly, that kind of focus is the solution to a lot of the mistakes entrepreneurs make when they start to grow their business. Don't let yourself get distracted chasing opportunities or adding new ideas. Hone in on what's made you successful so far and double down on that. That's the best way to set yourself up for sustainable, scalable success.

Key Takeaways:

- **Boredom means you're winning**: Steady revenue and routine operations aren't sexy, but they're signs of success. Don't chase shiny new things just because you're bored.

- **I had it backward**: I spent tens of thousands adding brick-and-mortar to my successful e-commerce business while those companies were desperately trying to sell online. Comparison warps your thinking.

- **More leads to less**: Too many commitments mean you can't focus on any of them. The overwhelm trap creeps up gradually until you're paralyzed.

- **The overwhelm fix**: Pause 24–48 hours, sort tasks into must/should/could, pick ONE focus, and tame your list before adding anything new.

The Teenage & Empty Nester Phases: Raising a Business that Runs Without You

The teenage years are bittersweet. It's exciting to watch your kid discover their passions and become independent. It's also a weird mix of grief and relief when you realize they don't need you the same way anymore. Your role shifts. In some ways, it's easier. No more constant oversight. But there are new challenges as your kids grapple with bigger questions and test their independence.

A similar shift happens when your business is fully established and ready to scale. You need to strike a tricky balance. At this stage, you can't be hands-on with everything, but you also can't over-delegate and lose touch with critical operations. Making the shift from on-the-ground manager to big-picture visionary isn't always smooth. And once you reach this stage, you have options. Keep scaling bigger or stay at your current revenue level? Stay involved full-time or hire a team to handle day-to-day operations? Sell the business and move on to something new? There's no one right answer, but you need to find your answer once your business has a solid foundation that lets it run without you.

This section helps you figure that out. We'll cover scaling strategies—refining your concept, developing the right founder mindset, building systems and teams to support growth. Getting a business to this point takes a toll on founders, and that can become the roadblock to future success if you don't address it. That's why I've included chapters on resilience, recovery, and building community; all are necessary if you want to keep operating at a high level.

CHAPTER 17

Is Your Business Scalable? (A Hard Look)

Let's start with a truth that might be kind of hard to hear at first: just because a business is profitable doesn't mean it's guaranteed to scale successfully. Scaling isn't just a matter of cranking up the marketing dial and hiring a bigger team. Some business concepts are best suited to staying small. Even with the ones that are easier to scale, there are more differences between a $100,000 business and a $10 million one than just their revenue.

So what makes a business scalable? Two main things. One, it has a big enough audience for you to substantially grow your customer base. Marketing is useless if you don't have anyone to reach. If you've already maxed out the demand for what you do, growing bigger just isn't realistic, at least, not with what you're currently offering. But that leads to the second thing that makes a concept scalable: if you can add revenue streams.

We've been focusing on that second area over the last five years at RSG Sales. The pandemic really drove home how important it is to have more than one way to make money, and we've made a concentrated effort to build them into our business. We're not just doing account management anymore. Some customers just need the account and want to manage it themselves, so we added new account fees and paid training on how to best manage sales with online retailers. That's two new revenue streams right there. We also have connections with people who place products in brick-and-mortar stores. That's not a side of the business we want to get hands-on with, but we turned these connections into partnerships. Now, we get a share of revenue when we connect a client with those companies, and add another revenue stream in the process.

Most businesses that scale do it by using both those strategies. They add products or services and expand their customer base. Figuring out how to balance these types of growth starts with some deep thinking. For starters, focus on your current customers. Is there anything they often need or ask for that you don't do now, but could? You can also look at your competitors. What do they offer that you don't yet, and is that something you could add? From there, expand your focus. Who aren't your customers right now, but could be? And how can you connect with them?

This might mean expanding what types of customers you work with, not just where you look for them. To give an example, let's say you're an accounting firm specializing in established mid-sized software companies; one way to scale could be adding startups to your customer base, or going the other way and expanding into enterprise and corporate accounting. You could also start taking clients from adjacent industries. Maybe you could create teams focused on IT providers or IoT manufacturers.

If you run a brick-and-mortar, your physical space puts an upper limit on how many customers you can reasonably serve. Scaling past that limit is going to take more than just marketing. It could mean expanding your capacity with a second location, or turning your single shop into a franchise. But you could also grow through adding services or products. Maybe you could add a mobile service that takes care of clients in their own homes, or you could launch a line of related products. A shampoo line from a salon, or joint care supplements developed by a chiropractor.

The point here is that there are a lot of ways to scale a business concept, and you should think carefully about which ones are the best fit for not just your business, but also you and your family. Before you jump into your growth plans, play the tape out to get a full sense of what kind of investment you'll need to make in terms of money, time, and energy. For that salon, for instance, budget out how much you'd have to pay a new team of stylists and how many clients you'd need each of them to have to make the new location profitable. Also, think about how much time you can realistically shift over from family or personal time into the business, and how that will impact your home dynamic and stress levels. Growth for growth's sake isn't worth it if it means sacrificing your health or relationships.

I'll also repeat the warning I've given before against falling for the bright-and-shiny. Don't just add something because it's trendy or sounds like a cool idea. Make sure it actually makes sense for your business. Jim Cocks confessed to me that he's jumped at shiny opportunities before, and it's never paid off the way he wanted it to. Sustainable growth needs to be predictable and measured, which means having the discipline to say no to things that don't fit your model. Level Up has been growing consistently since 2019, even through all the economic craziness that's happened during that time, and Jim says this is because "we don't just chase what's sexy, we chase what works."

Palak Shah told me the same thing when I asked how she's scaled her business. What's worked best, she says, is "saying no to 90% of opportunities. We don't scale reactively; we scale strategically. If something doesn't fit the ecosystem, it's a distraction."

And here's a step that's necessary, even though it's likely going to be uncomfortable: figure out whether you can absorb the loss if your attempt to scale fails. I'm not saying you should plan for failure, but nothing in business is guaranteed. Run your numbers, factoring in your new costs. Can you still cover expenses? How will it impact your cash flow? Can you operate at a lower profit margin in the short term without damaging the foundation of your business?

Something else Palak Shah told me comes to mind here: that success isn't just about momentum, it's about insulation and clarity. As she says, "If your peace is entirely dependent on performance, you've built something fragile." And if your business is fragile, you don't want to put extra strain on it by scaling. That's why she focused on building wealth first. By the time she was ready to grow, she had a stable foundation of assets to support it. That meant she could make strategic decisions from a place of power instead of needing to make quick moves under pressure.

It costs money to scale, however you go about it, whether it's buying a new location or ramping up your marketing to expand your customer base. This makes it super important to know your numbers inside and out. And not just your sales and revenue. The metrics we talked about in previous chapters, like customer acquisition cost and lifetime customer value, are key in choosing the right marketing campaigns and outreach.

Knowing your numbers will also show you any problems your business has right now, so you can fix them first.

Your business should be close to perfect at its current size before you start to grow. You can't scale your way out of the red. If you're not making money doing what you're doing, don't try to scale. Same deal if you can't keep up with current demand, or if your retention sucks on either the employee or the customer side. Absolutely don't even think about scaling if you're still not paying yourself. Whatever problems are in your business today, scaling is more likely to multiply them than fix them.

A business is ready to grow when it's earning healthy margins, operating with a stable team using functional systems. Of course, so far I've been making a pretty big assumption: that you even want to scale in the first place.

The advice you'll get from coaches and blogs usually assumes you want to do this by default, and that can make founders feel like they need to scale to be successful. There's an unspoken assumption across the entrepreneurial world that if you're not constantly growing, you're somehow failing.

Let me start by busting that myth. Scaling your business is absolutely optional, and isn't something you should feel compelled to do unless it's actually the right move, not just for your business, but also in a broader sense for you as a human. There's also no deadline or timeline that you have to follow. Just because your business is theoretically ready to scale doesn't mean you need to do it right now. Maybe your family has a lot going on right now, and you can just manage your business at its current size and scope. If growing more would overwhelm you, or even if you just like where you are and don't want to disrupt that balance just yet, that's completely valid, and you shouldn't feel like you need to keep growing just to do it.

Our business culture is obsessed with scaling. The overarching message is that bigger is better, and if you're not growing, you're dying. But let's pause a minute and think about where this obsession comes from. A lot of it stems from an investor mindset. The venture capital world needs businesses to scale exponentially for their model to work. But since most of us aren't VC-backed in the first place, there's no reason to adopt their metrics.

I think social media plays into this a lot, too. We see the celebrations of massive growth, and that whets the ego's appetite. Business growth becomes a kind of status symbol. Saying "I run a business with 8-figure yearly revenue" sounds more impressive than "I run a profitable business that gives me freedom." But what you don't see on that highlight reel is the toll scaling has taken on the owner's health, relationships, and quality of life. The person running the steady, stable business might actually be happier and able to enjoy their life more than the one constantly striving for more, so deciding which of them is more "successful" comes down as much to how you define success as what they've actually achieved.

All of this is to say there are valid reasons to keep a successful business at its current size. I already touched on work-life balance and family priorities. A bigger business often means more stress, more hours, less freedom, and less time for the people who matter most. There are also business cases for staying at your current size. The bigger you are, the harder it is to maintain consistent quality. There's profound satisfaction in knowing you do your job extremely well, instead of constantly climbing up new learning curves. Staying smaller also often means lower overhead and less financial pressure, so you can keep earning a solid revenue without as much financial risk.

Scaling a business costs more than just money, too. More people mean more complexity, more communication challenges, and more HR issues. You'll also likely need to overhaul your systems because what worked in a small operation often breaks under growth. Then there are the shifts to your role as the owner. Scaling means pivoting from doing the work to managing people who do the work, and not everybody wants to make this transition.

Personally, I've reached a stage in my life where I don't want to scale another business. I'm passionate about RSG Sales, and I want it to keep thriving, but that doesn't need to mean it gets any bigger than it is right now. I don't need to prove anything to myself or anyone else.

After building several businesses, closing one, and selling another, I've learned a few things that I wish I'd understood earlier. For one thing: success is personal. Only you can define what success looks like for you. Not online business gurus, not your business coach, not your peers, not even your family. Your definition of success is also likely to change over time. What's right for you at 30 might not be a good fit when you're 40 or 50. It's natural for your business to evolve along with you.

I had a seven-figure exit when I sold E by Design, which looks pretty impressive on paper. But there's no space on that ledger for missed games, 3 a.m. email sessions, and constant pressure. Were those things worth it? In many ways, yes. Would I do it again? Not a chance. I look back at the younger me who was constantly pushing for bigger, more, and faster, and I want to ask her: What do you really want?

Before you take any steps to scale your business, I want you to ask yourself that same question. Don't think about what others expect, or what you "should" do. Think hard about what sparks your passion and joy. What successes are you the most proud of? What would you do even if you weren't being paid, and what parts of your work make you lose track of time? That's a sign you're doing something you love.

One last tip I'll give here is that scaling isn't the only way to keep your business moving forward. Just because you're not actively growing doesn't mean you've gone stagnant or complacent. Instead of making your business bigger, you can focus on making it better. Fine-tune your operations, look for ways you can create more value for your clients, or think about services or products that don't fully serve your vision that you'd like to eliminate. These things can be the first step to scaling, but they don't have to be. They can be things you do for their own sake, to make your current business the best possible version of itself.

Key Takeaways:

- **Scaling is optional**: Bigger isn't always better. I don't need to scale RSG Sales anymore. I'm done proving things to myself or anyone else.

- **Know your numbers inside and out**: You can't scale your way out of the red. If you're not profitable now, don't try to grow. Fix the problems first.

- **Success is personal**: Only you define what success looks like. Not gurus, not coaches, not social media. And your definition will change over time.

- **The seven-figure exit lesson**: E by Design looked impressive on paper, but there's no ledger line for missed games and 3 a.m. emails. Was it worth it? In many ways, yes. Would I do it again? Not a chance.

CHAPTER 18

Thinking Like a CEO: The Shift that Changes Everything

Are your thought patterns helping you grow, or keeping you small? That's a question every entrepreneur should ask themselves when they want to grow their business, but it's not an easy one to answer. For one thing, it requires you to think about how you think (which is harder than it sounds). Then there's the tricky fact that the thought processes you've used to start and build your business usually need to evolve when you want to scale.

If you're feeling a bit lost here, let me share a story about the day I made a phone call that completely changed how I think about business, success, and most importantly, myself.

I was standing in the Toronto airport with my heart pounding, about to call Josh to tell him I'd just invested $25k in a mastermind program. Now, this might not sound revolutionary to you, but here's some context: I had NEVER invested in myself before. Period. The idea of spending that kind of money honestly terrified me at the moment, especially since I'd already stepped outside my comfort zone to reach that decision point.

The build-up to this moment started a few months before, when I attended a home decor industry conference in Charleston. There, I heard Eleanor Beaton speak, and something clicked. Finally, I heard from someone who actually understood what it meant to be a woman entrepreneur trying to scale a business. Two months later, I did something even more uncomfortable: I flew by myself to Toronto for her workshop. Hello, introvert anxiety! But that discomfort led me to learn exactly what I needed and pushed me to take this even bigger step of investing in her full program.

That $25k price tag for the program was a stretch for us financially. My immediate thought was "I shouldn't spend that kind of money on myself."

But I pushed through that and took the leap, and it turned out to be exactly what I needed to push me and my businesses to the next level.

This whole experience taught me something crucial. Sometimes, the very thinking that feels like it's protecting us is actually an anchor keeping us from growing. Instead of asking "Can I afford this?" I flipped my perspective and asked myself, "How will this help me grow?"

Because I made that mindset shift, when I was invited to join an elite program for multi-million-dollar business coaches and consultants, with a $60k a year price tag, my thinking had evolved. It was still scary, but I'd stopped worrying over what would happen if it didn't work. Instead, I could be excited about what would happen if it did.

That second program put me in rooms with people running $20M+ businesses, which, I'll admit, was very intimidating at first. What I discovered, though, was that these high achievers were just like me: fellow entrepreneurs wanting to learn and grow their business. The only difference was that they'd already done the mindset work I was just starting.

You don't need to join a program before you make this mental shift. You can start right now, in fact. The first step is checking in on your current thinking. Ask yourself: When was the last time you invested in yourself? What is your immediate reaction to spending money on your growth? Are you more inclined to justify investments in others than yourself?

When you don't invest in yourself, that puts the brakes on your business growth. You're more likely to underprice your services and miss growth opportunities because you stay in your comfort zone. That $25K phone call was the best scary decision I ever made. Not only did it force me into a much-needed mental shift, but it also expanded my network to include other successful business owners, a valuable source of knowledge and support.

Of course, just like with any investment, you want to put your money into things that will give you a real return. I came across that first mastermind program through a series of fortunate events, operating purely on gut instinct (and a healthy dose of nervous energy). Since then, I've developed a more strategic way to find and evaluate opportunities, and I've learned that having a system makes these decisions less scary.

Step one is to clarify your immediate reaction, on a scale from 1 (total panic) to 5 (excited about the possibilities). What are your first thoughts about the cost? Does the timeline feel comfortable? Are you confident in the program, and are you ready for a change? Once you know where you stand, take a close look at the opportunity itself to gauge its potential return on what you invest. Use a similar scale of 1 (minimal impact) to 5 (game-changing potential) to rate how it could impact your revenue growth, skill development, network, systems, market positioning, and team.

The last thing is to think about the risks involved. What will you need to sacrifice to take advantage of the opportunity? Again, think about this across all areas of your life, from financial stability to your time and the potential impact on your family.

If your scores are mostly in the 3-5 range, then that's a sign the opportunity is at least worth looking at more closely. The next step is to decide if it's what your business needs right now. Identify the current growth blockers in your business and what key skills you need to overcome them. Will the program you're considering help in those areas? How much will you need to grow your revenue to make it worth the time and expense, and does that seem like a boost you can realistically get from making the investment? Also, think about your current capacity. Can you add more to your plate without driving yourself insane, or if not, could your team or family step up to take on extra tasks so you can shift some time and energy into self-improvement?

When I was considering the $60K elite mastermind program, my first response was "oh shit, now I have to tell Josh the price." But then I took a step back. I knew the program was credible because I'd already seen others benefiting with real results. I also knew I was ready to kick my business into a new gear. Revenue was strong but starting to plateau, and our biggest blocker was a limited high-level network, something I could get from this program. I also got a reality check from realizing I'd already made my investment back from the $25K program 10 times over.

What was really holding me back, I eventually realized, was the fear of uncertainty. That's something that plagues entrepreneurs in a lot of areas. It's the pit in your stomach when the economy shifts, the up-all-night worry about making payroll, the constant back-of-mind question: "What if this all falls apart?"

Here's something no one tells you about entrepreneurship: Sometimes, it gets really fucking scary.

Being a small business owner comes with inherent risks. Yes, you get to be your own boss and do something you're passionate about, but you also need to pay the mortgage and keep food on the table. No matter how carefully you build a solid foundation for your business, there's always the chance something outside your control will come along and knock it out from under you.

That's what happened to us when COVID hit. The trade shows that were our only source of leads shut down overnight, and all our existing clients were facing insane shipping costs that ended up putting about half of them out of business. Everything we had built was under threat. I'd love to tell you I was calm and collected, with a contingency plan already in place, but the truth is I was terrified. We had three kids depending on our business and no clear path forward. The fear of failure felt overwhelming and not an option.

Every entrepreneur I know has been in a situation like this at least once. When I asked Jim Cocks if he's ever felt like giving up, his response was an instant, "Oh yeah. I've had moments where I just want to blow the whole thing up, move off-grid, and live on $500 a month with zero responsibilities." What he's learned, though, is that those feelings are a signal that something needs to shift in his strategy, mindset, or team dynamic. The key, he says, "is to not act on the emotion. Process it. Then ask: what needs to change so this feels aligned again?"

That's basically how we got through our panic moment at RSG Sales. Instead of letting it paralyze us, we used it as a springboard into a big pivot. Launching our YouTube channel put us on the world e-commerce stage, and our client base exploded with businesses all over the world who wanted to reach the U.S. market. We also looked at our numbers in a new way, figuring out the minimum income we needed for family essentials, the business costs that were absolutely necessary, and which things we could do without until we righted the ship.

We did the same kind of interrogation of our systems and customer base. Which parts of our business model are working? How can we reallocate resources toward different opportunities? What customer needs still exist, or what new ones are emerging? The answers to these questions helped us see that, while trade shows were gone, the need for e-commerce expertise was greater than ever. This told us it was worth it to take a calculated risk with our YouTube channel.

The bottom line here: How you handle uncertainty is often what determines whether your business stagnates, fails, or transforms into something even better. The most powerful shift happens when you don't see "failure" as an ending but instead take it as market feedback. Every challenge gives you insight into what works, what doesn't, and what you can do differently.

Of course, even knowing that doesn't stop these moments from being incredibly stressful and scary when you face them. Wrangling those emotions starts by separating your personal worth from your business. A business setback doesn't make you a failure as a person or a parent. In fact, your kids will learn more from watching you navigate challenges than they ever would from only seeing you succeed.

These moments are also when it becomes absolutely essential to have some stress management techniques in place. Jade Green has had moments when she spirals. Without a partner to fall back on if something goes wrong, she knows that, if she doesn't show up, the money doesn't come in. She has a set of tools she relies on when this happens, like meditation and breathwork. She's also studied flow state to learn how to regulate her nervous system, reset her brain, and keep burnout at bay, which has been huge for her to manage stress and show up at her best. Lately, to trigger flow state, she's been relying on something unexpected: snowboarding. It's an exercise in staying calm under pressure and making fast decisions, and as she says, "All of that helps me focus better and show up sharper when I'm back at my desk."

Being an entrepreneur means living with uncertainty, but it also means having the freedom to create your own solutions. We're facing some uncertainty again right now with RSG Sales in the face of tariffs and the shifts they're triggering in the global economy. The truth is, the cycle of business uncertainty never really ends, but over time, you get better at navigating it. And sometimes, what feels like a desperate move born from fear becomes the best business decision you've made yet.

Key Takeaways:

- **Invest in yourself to unlock growth**: That terrifying $25K mastermind call from Toronto changed everything. Stop waiting for permission to bet on yourself.

- **Ask better questions**: Instead of "Can I afford this?" ask "How will this help me grow?" That mindset shift is what let me say yes to the $60K program.

- **Uncertainty is the job**: COVID killed our only lead source. We pivoted to YouTube and exploded. How you handle uncertainty determines if you stagnate or transform.

- **Your worth isn't your business**: Separate personal failure from business setbacks. Every challenge is just market feedback showing you what to do differently.

CHAPTER 19

The Black Friday That Broke My Systems

I can just see your eyes rolling back in your head. More systems. Remember, systems aren't sexy, but they are meant to make your life and the life of your team easier. That's their one job.

The difference when you're talking about a large company is that the volume of tasks you need to tackle is higher, which makes it even more important to have systems that are as efficient as possible. The less time, thought, and energy you need to put into any given task, the better; which, again, is always true, but something you'll notice much more when you do something 50 times a day instead of five.

There's another side to this, too. It's not just that a system should cut down on the mental and physical energy you need to invest in tasks. The system itself shouldn't require much thought or effort, either. This is why, once you're at the point of scaling, you're very often going to be looking at third-party software instead of manual systems you develop in-house.

In fact, you'll probably start replacing any manual systems you used as a start-up with software equivalents before you start to scale, especially for repetitive tasks that are at the core of your business. Examples of these would be things like booking software for a salon or house cleaning business, or fulfillment and invoicing for sellers of physical products; the stuff that's routine but necessary for you to make revenue, and that you need to do more of to scale.

A lot of business software is designed to grow with its customers' companies. A common model is to have a free or low-cost version that's bare-bones but does everything you need as a startup. Once you outgrow the free version, you can upgrade to a higher tier to unlock higher sales or customer volumes, add more features and reports, or make use of more sophisticated customization so you can shape the software to do exactly what you need it to.

Something else you'll often unlock when you upgrade your software is more automation, and that can be a game-changer when you're scaling. The goal is to have as few human touches as possible with most of the tasks in your business, so that you and your team can focus on things like strategy and client relationships, the things that really grow revenue long-term. Automation lets you multiply your business significantly without needing to add employees, and that's good news when you're scaling from both a profit margin and a complexity standpoint.

I've been talking in really vague terms here because every business's journey is going to be a little different. For service or client-based businesses, upgrading from manual sales and customer tracking to CRM software is necessary if you want to scale. On the other hand, product sellers focused on volume will want to invest in things like marketing software and programs that track and manage their inventory, sales, and fulfillment. A CRM might still be useful, but it's not as integral to your operations as those other things mentioned.

Let me explain what I did at E by Design. It might make all of this make more sense. When we started, I processed orders, inventory, and invoices by hand. This blew up in my face on our first Black Friday. All five members of my family spent three days processing orders. This is how I knew without a shadow of a doubt that I needed a new system.

After some research, I was able to work with a company that allowed me to automate the processing of orders and inventory by about 90%. The invoicing piece was what I called semi-automated. In other words, to complete the process, we still needed a human touch. Eventually, this also crashes because of order volume. I'm not complaining. It was a good problem to have. I went on a 6-month search for the right software that would solve all of the problems. Oh, and yes, we basically duct-taped the other programs to keep the train moving forward.

I finally landed on an ERP system that allowed me to customize exactly what E by Design needed. Fulfillment, invoicing, accounting, and inventory were all managed within the ERP. This investment in automation made selling E by Design so much easier because the automation attracted big buyers. That's the kind of efficiency you want when you're focused on scaling.

AI has a growing place in this conversation, too. Jim Cocks is one of many entrepreneurs I know who is leaning into AI hard and taking full advantage of its efficiency-boosting potential. At Level Up, they use an AI marketing assistant that helps with content and copywriting, and they are building AI into their lead generation as a way to qualify people before they even talk to a human. He's also created AI systems that answer questions for team members and clients. He explains, "We've got a sales assistant AI trained on everything I've ever taught, so the sales team can literally ask it questions in real time like 'How do I handle this objection?' And for our clients, we're launching an AI version of me, a 'Jim-bot', that pulls from our training and resources so they can get help any time, on demand."

One thing to remember here, though, is that Jim's not relying on AI for any core tasks. When I asked him what his most valuable systems are today, he said it's the "non-tangible ones. It's the internal processes we've built: how we onboard clients, manage projects, track metrics, and handle customer service, that make everything run."

Palak Shah took a similar approach to building her systems that I took with RSG Sales. As her real estate business grew, she layered in systems for asset management, cash flow tracking, and maintenance coordination. For her type of business, these are the core functions that are necessary but don't need a human touch. When I asked about her most valuable systems today, she said they're "tied to portfolio performance optimization, including refinance timing, equity growth strategies, and capital redeployment models." In other words, as her business has grown and become more sophisticated, the key systems she uses have followed suit.

Her priorities were different on the coaching side of her business. There, she started with client delivery. "We built airtight onboarding, curriculum flows, community engagement protocols, and support systems to ensure high-touch results at scale." Only after those were locked down did she move on to other areas. Like Jim, Palak has been selectively making use of AI to operate faster and smarter. "That said, we don't use AI to replace strategy or leadership. It's there to amplify our thinking, not substitute it. The goal is always to create more space for high-level work while maintaining a personalized, values-driven experience across every part of the business."

As you can see just from these three examples, all of us picked different systems as the first and most important ones to improve when we were scaling. There's not one right answer. It's really about which systems are going to break first, and that completely depends on your business.

It's time to upgrade a system when your old ones can't keep up with your current pace, and things start falling through the cracks. Another sign is if you're losing money or leaving revenue on the table because of the process you're using. Here's a tip from your business mentor: very often, these are going to be the same areas where you've experienced problems earlier in your business' lifecycle. If you want to get ahead of the game and upgrade systems proactively before they break, this can be a good way to go about it. Think about the areas where you've run into bottlenecks before, and optimize them as much as you're able.

Something else that's going to influence this process is how you plan to scale. Increasing leads and sales volume isn't the only way to go about it. At RSG Sales, for instance, we've scaled by focusing on high-level customers and increasing the total lifetime value of each account, rather than going for straight volume. If you're taking this route of niching down on high-ticket clients or products, then you may not need to put as much thought into systems aimed at lead generation or automating your customer or client management.

How much you need to scale your team is also going to vary. Some businesses do need to expand headcount as they scale, but others can grow to $1 million or more in revenue without a big team. When I sold E by Design, we still had a very small crew. There were just two of us on the business side of things, plus the designer and the fulfillment center. This made the business easy to sell once I decided I was ready to exit.

That's another point you should think about when you're setting up systems to scale. If you plan to sell the business, you need to set it up so that it can operate completely independently of any one person, including you as the owner. We've talked a bit already about why this is a smart idea for any business, but it's especially important if you know you want to step back in the near future. The more plug-and-play your business is for the buyer, the easier it's going to be to sell. This is part of why consulting businesses are very difficult to sell; their success relies a lot on the reputation and knowledge of a single individual.

I'll go into the nitty-gritty of scaling a team in the next chapter, but there's one other area related to scaling systems that I wanted to touch on before we get there, and that's the financial side of the equation.

Scaling costs money, however you go about it. Keeping your finances during and post-scaling starts with solid planning before it happens. In a sense, it's like recreating your business plan. You need to estimate your expenses moving forward and plot out exactly how you'll earn revenue to cover them before scaling the same way you did before you launched. This includes the market research side of figuring out whether the market is there to support your growth, what software, equipment, or employees you'll need to add to make it happen, and whether you can afford those additions.

If you need to add something expensive to reach the next level, like a new piece of equipment or another location, then deciding how you'll cover those up-front expenses is another key step. Even if you have enough cash on hand to pay for it outright, that might not be the best choice. If it'll deplete your reserves and leave you without a buffer for the unexpected, a bank loan or line of credit could end up being the most financially sound decision.

In some cases, scaling will require a deeper retooling of how you approach finances in general. I'll give an example here. I once worked with a product-based manufacturer that had operated for years by never taking out loans. They only bought what they could afford out-of-pocket. If they wanted a million-dollar piece of equipment, they had to pay for it in cash. That worked early on to keep them from taking on risky debt, but once they were ready to scale, this mindset was holding them back. It simply wasn't feasible to wait until they'd earned enough to cover the extensive equipment upgrades required to go to the next level. They'd also reached a point where such a conservative approach to debt wasn't necessary, now that they had more assets and an entire successful business backing their borrowing. Once the company made that mindset switch and embraced taking on selective, productive debt to grow, their revenue skyrocketed, and they reached a level of success they never could have with their old mindset.

Now, I'm not saying that you should just take out loans willy-nilly to cover things you can't afford. Since he's an accountant, Robert Patin understands financial management even better than most successful founders, and he gives excellent advice on this point. Before he invests in any new growth, he clarifies exactly what result he needs to see from it that will make it worth it. He sets two standards: a minimum expectation and an ideal outcome, with a defined deadline for when he'll achieve them. This keeps him from falling victim to sunk cost fallacy thinking. If his growth attempt falls short, if he doesn't get to his minimum by the deadline, he pulls back and reassesses. He also makes sure that he can afford to sacrifice both the financial and time capital he'll invest, even if he doesn't get the results he's hoping for. His recipe for sustainable, ongoing growth is "pick a direction, pick a timeline, pick an expectation, and have a direction of here's the decision I'm going to make and what the result needs to be." Doing this consistently for every decision has kept his business on an upward trajectory.

I'll end on one last piece of advice that homeowners will be able to relate to. Making investments in your business has one big thing in common with home renovations: you need to plan for the unexpected. There will always be something that costs more than you thought it would, or extra costs you don't think about until the project's already underway. When I implemented that business-in-a-box software in E by Design, for example, there were labor costs on top of the price of the software that I hadn't initially budgeted for. I ended up needing to hire people to set it up, customize it, and train us in how to use it. But I could absorb those unexpected costs because I'd planned for a contingency budget.

You always want to do the same thing when you're investing in new software, new equipment, a new location, or whatever else you need to scale. If you end up not using that extra budget, then that's great! You can put that money toward your next project. What you don't want is to get stuck partway through because the costs were higher than you'd planned for, and you run out of money.

Whether it's how you manage your finances or how your business runs day-to-day, scaling isn't just a matter of expanding your capacity. That's the end goal, but to reach it usually means making more substantial changes to how you think and operate. The specific steps you take to scale will be unique to your business, but the need to take those steps strategically is universal.

Key Takeaways:

- **Systems make life easier, period**: When things start falling through the cracks, it's time to upgrade. Don't wait until everything breaks.

- **Automate the routine stuff**: Fewer human touches on repetitive tasks means more time for strategy and client relationships - the things that actually grow revenue.

- **My Black Friday disaster**: All five family members spent three days processing orders by hand. Don't wait for your own crisis to fix your systems.

- **Always budget for the unexpected**: That ERP software had hidden costs for setup, customization, and training. Plan for 20–30% more than you think you'll need.

- **Fix problems before you scale**: You can't scale your way out of the red. Whatever's broken now will only multiply when you grow.

CHAPTER 20

Culture over Credentials: Scaling Smart

Here's something that might surprise you: you don't need a huge team to scale your business. In fact, some of the most profitable businesses I know have stayed intentionally small while growing their revenue significantly.

When I sold E by Design, we still had a very small crew. There were just two of us on the business side of things, plus the fulfillment center. I had already banked two years' worth of designs and future collections. This made the business incredibly profitable and easy to sell once I decided I was ready to exit. We'd built what I like to call a "small and mighty" team; each person was essential, skilled, and aligned with our vision.

The key to scaling with a small team isn't just about hiring fewer people. It's about hiring the right people and creating systems that multiply their impact. It's about being strategic rather than reactive when it comes to adding team members.

So how do you know when it's actually time to hire? Nick Rodsater has a data-driven approach that I really respect. He looks at metrics like revenue per employee, patient wait times, and patient visits versus their capacity. Their goal is to consistently be booked at 80–90% of capacity. If those numbers creep up over 90% and stay there, that's a sign it's time to hire. He also uses what he calls a team capacity tachometer, where employees score their capacity to perform to their full ability on a 0–100 scale.

Jade Green takes a different approach, and one that honestly resonates with me more. When I talked to her, she was considering hiring an operations lead but was hesitant. The reason? "I didn't want to commit to building something physical again if it meant compromising my freedom," she said. Her advice is that if you're not willing to do the work to set your team up for success with clear job descriptions, expectations, and accountability, then you shouldn't hire, "because hiring a team means showing up."

That last part is crucial. Hiring someone isn't just about delegating tasks off your plate. It's about taking on the responsibility of leadership, which is a whole different skill set.

When you do decide to hire, here's what I've learned matters most: culture fit trumps skills every single time. Jim Cocks puts it perfectly: "Skills can be taught, but values, work ethic, and integrity can't. I've made the mistake of hiring someone who looked amazing on paper but didn't align with our culture, and it ended in disaster."

This is where a lot of entrepreneurs get tripped up, especially as they scale. You start bringing people in based on their resume or technical abilities, but you don't pay enough attention to whether they actually fit with the culture you've built. And here's the thing: your culture becomes more defined as your business matures. What might have worked in the scrappy startup days might not work when you're trying to serve high-end clients or manage complex systems.

So how do you maintain your culture and values as you add team members and increase revenue? It starts with being crystal clear about what those values actually are. Not the generic "integrity and excellence" stuff you see on corporate websites, but the real, lived values that guide how you actually operate.

At RSG Sales, for example, one of our core values is direct communication. We don't sugarcoat things or dance around problems. When someone joins our team, we make it clear that we value honest feedback and expect people to speak up when something isn't working. If someone's communication style is more passive-aggressive or conflict-avoidant, they're probably not going to thrive with us, no matter how skilled they are.

Nick Rodsater has a great approach to this. He says, "If someone isn't bought into the vision but we believe they have the right values, we work hard to identify where there may be a rub or contradiction and get everyone back on the same page. If we can't get things back in alignment, then it's time to make a change."

The key is being proactive about culture rather than hoping it will just happen naturally. As you grow, you need to be intentional about reinforcing your values through your hiring process, your onboarding, and your day-to-day operations. It's not enough to mention your values once during orientation and hope people remember them.

One of the biggest shifts you'll need to make as you scale is evolving your own role as the founder. A lot of those hats you wore to lead a startup are going to fit better on other people's heads as your revenue grows. The general shift should be away from hands-on operational tasks and toward more strategic planning. You might still get down in the weeds from time to time, but the bigger your business gets, the more of your time should be spent taking a top-down, big-picture view and leaving those day-to-day details to your team.

This is harder than it sounds, especially if you're a control freak like me. But here's what I learned: you're hiring people for their expertise. As the founder, you still give them the overall plan and direction, but beyond that, you need to step back and let them do what they do best.

With E by Design, for example, one of the biggest strengths I brought to the table was that I understood the market. Because of that, even though I had a designer, I always picked the final collections. That's one of the areas where I had a strong vision, which meant that it was a place I belonged as a founder. On the other hand, I got order processing off my plate literally as soon as I could. That was the kind of work that bogged me down and that I could be perfectly happy never needing to think about again.

Before you build out your team, think about where your passion and vision are strongest. It doesn't always mean you only work on high-level, strategic tasks. If you're a coach, for example, maybe you're excellent at working with clients, and that's the work you started your business to do. If that's the case, you don't want to scale yourself out of that. Maybe your approach to team building is to keep yourself in that deliverable stage and hire a Chief Operations Officer to take over the bulk of the behind-the-scenes work.

You can approach the question of who you need to hire in a similar way to how we talked about scaling systems in the last chapter. Think about the areas where you've run into the most bottlenecks from a time and skills standpoint, and hire the people who will solve those problems first.

When it comes to your first high-level leadership hire, 90% of the time, that's going to be an Ops Manager or COO; someone who excels at managing all the day-to-day tasks and work that needs to happen to keep the business running smoothly. That's the kind of hire that can really unlock your business's potential because they give you freedom to shift your attention away from the everyday and toward high-level planning and strategy.

There's a mindset shift involved in leadership that Palak Shah learned the hard way, and honestly, her mistakes sound very familiar because they're things I struggled with, too. She was afraid of being disliked and avoided tough conversations. Her mistake, she says, wasn't delaying hiring, but "not realizing how much leadership required of me personally. I over-accommodated instead of holding people to high standards. What I've learned since is that clarity and accountability are forms of respect. The more clearly I lead, the better my team performs, and the more trust we build."

This is so important. Being a good leader doesn't mean being everyone's friend. It means being clear about expectations, holding people accountable, and having the tough conversations when things aren't working.

Which brings me to the part of scaling that nobody likes to talk about: sometimes you have to let people go.

I'm not going to sugarcoat it; firing people sucks. I don't think anybody enjoys doing it. It's especially hard when you like the employee, and they're generally competent, but just don't have the skills or mindset your team needs to keep growing.

Unfortunately, this is also a situation that many business leaders have to deal with as they scale. Your business changes as it grows. Some employees will adapt and grow with you. With others, you'll start to see they don't fit as well in the current version of the company as they did when you hired them.

A few years ago, I talked my friend A. through just this kind of scenario. She had a team of about 15 people at the time, and they were "like family" (those dreaded words). The problem was, my friend's business just didn't bring in the revenue to support a team that large. So I gave it to her straight: her business couldn't keep supporting team members who weren't pulling their weight.

That was hard for her to hear, but she listened. She was quickly able to identify a few employees that she'd kept on the payroll because they'd been with her for a long time, but that she didn't really need. After she let those employees go, she called me in tears. Firing them had been hard, but she felt lighter now that she'd done it. It wasn't just relief that her numbers would improve. She felt better because she was finally being honest with herself, her team members, and her business.

It's not always easy to recognize when an employee doesn't fit your team anymore. I've learned to keep an eye out for a few signs. One is if they're not willing to adapt and update their skills as their role changes. Another sign is if you're constantly double-checking or correcting an employee's work, or if they seem overwhelmed by growing responsibilities.

As your culture gets more defined, you might also realize early hires don't align with it anymore. It could be that there's always tension with their coworkers, or that they have a negative attitude when it comes to growth or change.

If you think the employee could turn things around, you can start with a conversation. Be crystal clear about what you expect from them and where you feel they're falling short. Give them training or resources to help them level up to where you need them to be, and create a structured Performance Improvement Plan with clear milestones and timelines. I'll be honest, though; I've seen very few people stay at a company for long after a PIP is in place, so once you get to this point, the writing is usually already on the wall.

Jim Cocks has a perspective on this that I think is healthy: "The key thing I've learned is that team members are transient. Especially in support roles, people are going to move on, and that's okay. What's important is having a strong culture of growth and feedback so your people feel like they're evolving. If you can do that, you'll retain good talent longer."

Not every business will need to build a big team, but it's a rare company that can scale to $1 million or higher without hiring somebody. The key is being strategic about who you hire, when you hire them, and how you maintain your culture as you grow. Build a small and mighty team, not a large and chaotic one.

Key Takeaways:

- **Build small and mighty, not large and chaotic**: When I sold E by Design, we had just two people on the business side, plus our design team and fulfillment center. Stay lean and strategic.

- **Culture fit trumps skills every time**: Skills can be taught. Values, work ethic, and integrity can't. Hire people who align with how you actually operate, not just impressive resumes.

- **Your role evolves as you scale**: Figure out where your passion and vision are strongest, then hire people to handle everything else. I kept final collection decisions at E by Design, but got order processing off my plate immediately.

- **Maintain culture as you grow**: Be crystal clear about your actual values (not generic corporate BS) and reinforce them through hiring, onboarding, and daily operations.

- **Sometimes you have to let people go**: Your business changes as it grows. Some employees will adapt, others won't. Being honest about misalignment is better for everyone than dragging it out.

CHAPTER 21

Why You're Overwhelmed (and What to Do About It That Actually Works)

Let me paint you a picture of what overwhelm looks like in real time.

It's 2:47 p.m. on a Tuesday. You've been "working" since 6 a.m. Your to-do list has somehow grown longer despite the fact that you've been busy all day. You've attended three Zoom calls, answered approximately 847 emails, posted on social media, listened to a podcast about marketing funnels, and signed up for yet another course that promises to solve all your problems. You feel exhausted and productive at the same time.

Except here's the thing: you haven't actually done anything that moves your business forward. Not really.

Welcome to the Busy-Not-Productive trap, and it's one of the biggest reasons entrepreneurs find themselves overwhelmed as they try to scale.

Here's what nobody tells you about business growth: everything gets bigger, including your potential to make bigger, costlier mistakes. You'll be juggling more accounts, a wider range of services, and a higher volume of work. But the real problem isn't the volume; it's that most entrepreneurs are operating based on some fundamental misconceptions about how growth actually works.

I talked about the overwhelm trap in Chapter 16, but now I want to dig into the root causes that lead you into that trap in the first place. Because unless you address these foundational mistakes, you'll keep finding yourself back in the same exhausting cycle.

Let's start with the most common culprit: confusing motion with progress.

We've been conditioned to equate busyness with productivity. You want to grow your business, so your first impulse is to add more. More calls, more networking events, more content, more courses. But here's the brutal truth: a significant portion of what's filling your calendar is motion, not progress. It keeps you busy but doesn't actually move you toward your goals.

I get why this happens. Motion feels productive without requiring the discomfort of deep focus or the vulnerability of actual delivery. It's way easier to sign up for another course than to implement what you learned from the last three you took. It's more comfortable to attend another networking event than to follow up thoroughly with the connections you already made.

I made this exact mistake with RSG Sales when we were struggling to grow. I kept stacking on marketing activities, convinced that more visibility was the answer. I did podcasts, speaking engagements, and ramped up posting on every social media platform you can name. Did any of that actually move the needle? Not really. What finally worked was focusing deeply on converting the leads we already had and delivering exceptional results that generated referrals.

This leads perfectly into the next mistake that keeps entrepreneurs overwhelmed: Bright and Shiny Syndrome.

This is when you constantly chase new strategies instead of sticking with fundamentally sound ones long enough to see results. You try email marketing for three weeks, don't see immediate results, and jump to Instagram. A month later, you're pivoting to YouTube. Then you're exploring TikTok because someone told you that's where your audience is now. None of these platforms ever gets a real chance to work because you never stick around long enough to master them.

This happens all the time, especially when you're advertising a product or service. You run ads on Facebook for two weeks, spend $500, get a handful of clicks but no conversions, and immediately decide Facebook ads don't work. So you switch to Google Ads. Same story. Then you try Instagram. Before you know it, you've spent thousands of dollars and countless hours without giving any single approach enough time or optimization to actually succeed.

There's another root cause of overwhelm that's even more insidious, and that's underestimating the true cost of complexity. Every product line, marketing channel, or service you add doesn't just need the visible resources you allocate to it. There's a massive amount of invisible mental bandwidth that comes with it.

Decision fatigue from juggling multiple priorities. Cognitive load from maintaining different systems and processes. The mental strain of context-switching between projects. The emotional energy spent managing various stakeholder expectations. These hidden costs add up fast and can absolutely sink your productivity and mental health.

When we launched a second service line at RSG Sales, I calculated the direct costs: what we'd need to spend on marketing and what resources we'd need to deliver it. What I completely missed were these hidden costs. The result? Both service lines suffered because neither got the focused attention it needed. I was spreading myself so thin trying to manage both that I wasn't doing either one well.

If any of this sounds familiar, I have some good news: there are systems you can put in place to prevent these mistakes before they derail you.

The most useful one for me has been creating a standardized decision filter that every potential opportunity has to pass through before I commit. My filter asks five key questions:

- **Does this directly support my one primary focus for this quarter?** If not, it's an automatic "not right now."

- **Will this require more than 5% of my available working hours?** If yes, what specific thing will I stop doing to accommodate it?

- **Does this leverage my unique strengths, or will it pull me into areas of weakness?** Tasks in our weakness zones consume way more energy than things we're naturally good at.

- **Will I still be enthusiastic about this commitment in 30 days?** This helps identify "excitement bias" before it influences my decisions. That shiny new marketing strategy might seem amazing today, but will you still want to be managing it a month from now?

- **What would my future self wish I had decided?** This creates helpful distance and perspective when you're tempted by something new.

Passing opportunities through these five questions has saved me from countless instances of overcommitment. They remove the in-the-moment emotions and force me to think through the full ramifications of saying yes to whatever bright-and-shiny thing is catching my attention.

I also use what I call the "one in, one out" rule to contain the natural complexity that grows in any business. Before I add any new offer, marketing channel, or business component, I have to identify what I'll simplify or remove to maintain equilibrium. You can't just keep adding without taking anything away; that's how you end up with a bloated, unmanageable business that exhausts you.

I pair this with a quarterly complexity audit. Every three months, I review the business looking for redundant tools or systems, processes with too many steps, decision points that could be standardized, or services and products with low ROI compared to their complexity.

One entrepreneur I worked with did this audit and discovered her most profitable service was also her simplest to deliver. So she doubled down on that service and phased out three more complex ones. The result? Her profit increased, and her workload dropped by almost 40%.

The point here isn't to stop growing or trying new things. The point is to be strategic about what you take on and honest about what you need to let go. Because the truth is, most overwhelm doesn't come from doing too much of the right things; it comes from doing too much of everything.

As your business scales, your focus as the founder is naturally going to tighten. This is another area where I sometimes see entrepreneurs stumble, because it's not always obvious which things you should keep on your plate and which you should shift to someone else's. Palak Shah told me she made this mistake when she was growing her business. At one point, she realized she'd scaled herself out of coaching and creating, the main things she actually liked doing. Instead, she found herself spending all her time solving backend problems and managing operations. The business was thriving, but she was struggling. As she explains, "I had built something that no longer felt good to run. I didn't like how I was spending my days. It wasn't energizing anymore."

So she took a step back, leaned on her partner, and reached out to some mentors she trusted. Together, they reassessed the business and made some strategic restructuring decisions to bring Palak back into alignment with the work that she loves. Her advice to other business owners who hit this kind of wall is that it's a signal, "Not to quit, but to evolve. The biggest threat to your growth isn't failure; it's success that traps you. When that moment comes, don't double down. Redesign. Audit what's no longer serving you and ask: if I were building this from scratch, what would I keep?"

There's another common mistake that can lead entrepreneurs to fill their schedules with work they don't really want to do. I call it the "Everything Will Fall Apart" trap, AKA "Being the Human Duct Tape." This is another one I've personally fallen victim to. I have the terrible habit of asking myself, "If I don't do it, who will?" I cringe as I write this because it's a habit I've spent decades trying to break. This belief that if you step back, everything will crumble can keep you stuck in an exhausting cycle, where you're convinced that you're the only thing standing between order and chaos.

Entrepreneurs don't only fall into this mindset because they're control freaks (although, let's be real, we probably are). It's a learned habit more than anything. We've spent years being the reliable one everyone else comes to when stuff needs to get done. Most of us have seen what happens when we don't step in, too. Your brain pulls up that time you didn't double-check a client's deliverable, and there was a mistake, or when you didn't remind your teenager about their project, and they had to pull their first all-nighter. These examples become proof that your intervention is essential. There's also that lurking fear that if something does go wrong and you weren't there to prevent it, it'll be your fault. So, you might as well just handle everything yourself, right?

I won't tell you that everything will definitely be fine if you don't intervene. Most things will, but there will also be mistakes you don't catch, or work that doesn't get done without you nagging. Here's the thing, though: sometimes, that's exactly what needs to happen. There are times when things need to fall apart a little so they can be rebuilt better.

I know that sounds terrifying, but stick with me, because there's good news, too. Even when things go wrong, it's rarely the catastrophic disaster you imagined. The actual consequences are usually much more manageable, and the good things that happen when you step back make them worth it. In my experiments with relinquishing control, I've found that people rise to the occasion more often than they fall. When I stopped being the only one to handle client issues, my team developed stronger problem-solving skills; something they wouldn't have done if I stayed "indispensable." Best of all, when you're not solving everything, other people often come up with even better solutions that you never would have thought of. And, in the course of letting things fall apart, you learn exactly what areas do need your attention so you can focus your energy where your unique skills and perspective make the biggest impact.

And there's a cost to the human duct tape mindset, too. When every decision or process requires your input, you end up building a business that can't run without you. You also rob your team members (or kids, on the family side) of the chance to develop their own skills and learn from their own mistakes. You never discover what other people are capable of when you always control the outcome. Instead, you teach them that they can't function without you, and that sets you up for the kind of exhaustion and burnout that means you aren't able to show up at your best, either.

I'm not saying you should just abandon ship and hope for the best. The best fix for this mistake is to step back strategically, in a way that minimizes chaos and maximizes learning. Start small with one low-stakes area and deliberately don't take control. Instead, tell people your expectations and what the end result should look like, then let your team (or partner, or kids) figure out the rest. When things don't go perfectly, fight the impulse to retake control. Instead, work with whoever owns that task to help them figure out where things went awry and what they should do differently next time.

There's another common mindset mistake I see entrepreneurs make that I want to highlight before wrapping up this chapter, and that's the idea that discipline and willpower are magic fixes for an overfilled schedule. The myth that "more discipline equals more time" can absolutely sabotage your business because it sends you into a guilt spiral and keeps you stuck in an exhausting cycle. Instead of asking "Why is this harder than it needs to be?" you try to just power through it, or blame yourself for not being efficient or dedicated enough. As a result, you never take a step back to audit your systems and figure out which ones aren't working.

Parent entrepreneurs are especially likely to fall into this trap. Often, it's because you're using productivity systems that are designed for people with predictable schedules and uninterrupted work time. They're not made to adapt to doing 20-minute chunks of work between school pickup and soccer practice, or a morning routine that's blown up when your kid wakes up puking from a stomach flu. What you need to navigate this kind of chaos isn't discipline. It's clearer priorities, better boundaries, and systems that match your energy. No amount of discipline will fix a schedule with zero white space. To do that, you need systems that automatically protect your time, and to be honest about what actually matters, so you can let other things go when life intervenes. Instead of forcing yourself to do your hardest work when you're running on fumes, try designing your day around when you actually have energy. Build systems that give you permission to be human. Yes, some days you're going to choose your kid's science project over your business plan. That's not a lack of discipline; it's being a good parent. If your systems don't account for this reality, they're not the right systems for you.

I'm guessing most people reading this have made (or are currently making) some of these mistakes. Odds are, you'll probably make at least one of them again, and that's okay. As entrepreneurs, we can get a bit obsessed with optimizing and improving everything, and can start to beat ourselves up when those fixes don't stick right away. But some lessons take longer to learn than others. Berating yourself doesn't make that learning happen any faster. It's great to have high standards, but it's simply not realistic to expect perfection from anyone, and that includes yourself.

I like what Jim Cocks told me when I asked what he'd change if he had a do-over button. He acknowledged there were some projects and hires he'd skip in hindsight, but also said that all of them helped him grow and gave him strategies he now uses to coach others. "Like that $2,000 website I built for a business that I was in for two weeks? Total fail—but now I've told that story to thousands of people, helping them avoid the same trap. The detours were the tuition. I wouldn't change a thing."

Whenever you make a mistake in your business, whether it's the first time you make it or the fiftieth, try to approach it with that same mindset. Even things that feel like huge setbacks in the moment can become springboards that move you forward as long as you learn from them.

Key Takeaways:

- **Motion isn't progress**: Being busy doesn't mean you're actually moving your business forward. Attending three networking events beats implementing what you learned from one.

- **Cure your Bright and Shiny Syndrome**: Stop jumping platforms every two weeks. You're not giving any strategy enough time to actually work. Stick with fundamentals and get better at them.

- **Complexity has hidden costs**: Every new offer, marketing channel, or service drains mental bandwidth through decision fatigue, context-switching, and emotional energy - not just money.

- **Use a decision filter**: These five questions save me from constant overcommitment: Does this support my quarterly focus? What will I stop doing to make room? Will I still be enthusiastic in 30 days?

- **Let things fall apart strategically**: You're not indispensable. Step back in low-stakes areas and let your team figure it out. They'll rise to the occasion more often than they'll fail.

CHAPTER 22

Keeping Your Cup Full

You know that saying, "You can't pour from an empty cup"? It's a nice sentiment, but I absolutely hate that phrase. And it's also wrong. You can pour from an empty cup, it's just that nothing comes out.

Women from every walk of life know exactly what I mean. We've all poured from an empty cup, probably more times than we can remember. Which is masochistic, when you really stop to think about it, but I know why so many women—and especially moms, and most especially entrepreneur moms—keep doing this. We've been raised to believe that our worth is based on the service of others over ourselves, and programmed to think it's selfish to want more freedom or ease. Most of us learned early on that being "good" meant being helpful, not causing trouble, and making everyone else's life easier. We watched our mothers come home from work and start straight in on dinner, homework help, and managing everybody else's life before collapsing into bed exhausted, only to get up the next day and do it all again. In the process, we learned that this was what love looked like.

What nobody told us was that service without boundaries is self-destruction. When we operate from empty cups, we're not actually helping anyone. Instead, we're teaching everyone around us that our needs don't matter while burning ourselves out so completely that other people have to pick up the pieces. You end up making bad decisions for your business because you're too tired to make good ones, or snapping at your kids because you haven't had five minutes to yourself in three weeks. The truth is, as a business owner, taking care of yourself so you can show up at your best isn't selfish, it's strategic.

Here's something every parent entrepreneur needs to hear. You don't need to prove your worth by constantly working yourself to exhaustion. You don't need to earn the right to freedom and ease, or get anyone else's permission to live a life that feels good. You deserve rest, not because you've checked every box on every one else's list, but because rest is how humans function sustainably.

And as a corollary to this, when you have spent the last feels-like-forever pouring from an empty cup and end up with your batteries completely drained, there's nothing wrong with you. You don't need to fix yourself. You're just proving that you're human, and the "fix" is to give yourself the grace you'd give to anyone else.

I've been thinking a lot lately about why so many successful women immediately think we need to fix ourselves when we hit a rough patch. Probably because I've been in one myself. My dad had surgery in mid-2025, which added helping my parents to my already extensive list of reasons to stress. In the aftermath, I found myself immediately searching for "quick fixes" to get me out of the funk I was in. There's an entire industry that's built up around the idea that feeling unmotivated or tired is a problem that needs solving, exploiting the fact that women entrepreneurs, especially, have been conditioned to believe any dip in our energy means we're broken. Research shows that women are more likely than men to internalize stress and blame themselves when things feel hard. We're also more susceptible to emotional labor burnout from constantly managing not just our own feelings, but everyone else's, too.

Being an entrepreneur on top of this amplifies those feelings a thousand-fold. Business owners are used to identifying problems and creating solutions. We've built companies around making things better. Of course, we're going to treat our own emotional states like business problems that need solving. The obvious problem with this is that you're not a business problem. You're a human being having a human experience.

Your lack of motivation might not be a sign that something's broken. Maybe it's actually a signal that something's finally working, and your internal wisdom is telling you to slow down before you burn out completely. Instead of asking "How do I fix this?" the right question might be, "What is this trying to tell me?"

I've brought up a couple of times in this book that work-life balance is a myth. As parent entrepreneurs, it's just not realistic to find some perfect split where everything in your life gets equal attention. Instead, it's a matter of intentionally allocating your time based on what needs your attention right now. Unfortunately, when the business or kids or other family members need more time, that almost always gets shifted out of the area that's the easiest to view as "extra": the time you devote to taking care of yourself. This can work in the short-term, but eventually, your body and life are going to start sending you signs that you need to recalibrate and take some of that "you time" back.

What are those signs, you ask? There are a few I've learned to watch for. Some are physical: that you're getting sick more often, can't sleep even when you're exhausted, and feel like you're running on caffeine and willpower. There are emotional signs, too, like if you start to feel resentment building toward whatever is demanding the most from you, or you get that feeling that all of the things you're trying to juggle are about to come crashing down. Guilt is a strong signal. When I'm making choices based on what I think I should be giving time to instead of what actually needs attention most, I'm usually headed for a crash. The people in your life might start sending signals. For me, it's when Josh starts doing the thing where he asks "Are you okay?" more often than usual, the kids complain about never seeing me, and my team seems stressed and overworked. These are my signals. I've miscalculated somewhere and need to step back to reassess my time distribution. One of the biggest signs is when I find myself doing impossible math. If I'm trying to give the business 80%, my family 80%, and myself 80%, that's expecting myself to be roughly 2.4 humans, something that's just not possible, no matter how much willpower I pour into trying.

Of course, knowing it's time to recalibrate is just the first step. Where a lot of parent entrepreneurs feel completely lost is figuring out how to make those adjustments without anything falling apart. This is hard for many business owners because we're used to being self-sufficient and capable of tackling any challenge thrown our way. But self-sufficiency isn't the same thing as resilience. Every human has a breaking point. True resilience comes from knowing where yours is and creating systems and plans before you hit that point. Just because you can handle anything doesn't mean you should have to handle everything the same way. Self-sufficiency is about capability, but resilience is about sustainability.

What I've learned is that, as a self-sufficient person, I can handle almost any single crisis. But when multiple things hit at the same time: a child has a health scare while Josh is traveling, while RSG Sales is launching a new program, while my dad needs surgery, that's when I lean on the resilience systems I've developed. It isn't a lack of capability. It's recognizing that even capable people have limits. Systems take the emotional labor out of surviving these all-the-crises moments, taking some decisions out of your hands when your hands are already full.

Here's what my resilience system looks like in practice. First, I have the 72-hour rule. When something goes wrong, I give myself 72 hours to feel all the feelings. I can cry, rant to Josh, eat ice cream for breakfast; whatever needs to happen. After 72 hours, I shift into solution mode. It's not about suppressing emotions, but putting some boundaries around them before I enter a spiral.

Next is my Three-Person rule. I never make big decisions or process major setbacks on my own. There are three people I can call depending on what I need: someone who will be brutally honest (Josh), someone who will validate my feelings (my best friend), and someone who will help me see solutions (my business mentor). Having designated people means I don't need to guess who to reach out to when I'm in crisis mode.

I've also established my Minimum Viable Day. When things get extra hard, I have a list of the absolute minimum that needs to happen for it not to be a complete disaster. These are pure basics, like are the kids fed? Is everyone alive? Are all major client deadlines met? Some days that's enough, and having that baseline helps assuage the guilt about not doing more.

Knowing how to recognize my own stress signals is a big part of this, too. I have a sense for my canary-in-the-coal-mine moments, like when I'm checking email at 11 p.m. or snapping at the kids over small things. I have specific actions that I take when I notice these patterns.

Last, but far from least, I have systems to bounce back from difficult periods. It's the same way that athletes need recovery protocols after intense training. When you've pushed yourself to your limits physically, mentally, or emotionally (or all three), you can't just expect to carry on with business-as-usual without a reset. My list includes specific things like getting outside, calling a friend, or doing something creative. These are things I know can help me recharge and recenter.

I'm only mentioning a few specifics here because every person is different. Your crisis points and necessary boundary lines might be very different from mine, and the same is probably true for your best strategies to recover. I know from talking to fellow entrepreneur friends that each of them has their own approach to resilience. For Jade Green, it's all about intentional planning. Every weekend, she creates her ideal week to decide where her time and energy will go. Unexpected things might creep up and disrupt that, but as she says, "when you've mapped it out and communicated it to the people around you, you're far more likely to protect your time. That's how I create work-life alignment. Not by accident. By design."

Jade is also a big believer in active recovery and the importance of filling your cup with connection and quality time with family. "When you love what you do, you're going to be all in. You can't help it," she says. "But you also need to understand what that intensity does to your nervous system, your brain, and your body."

When I asked Jim Cocks how he manages the stress of owning a business, he answered, "I play a lot of video games. Seriously." He acknowledged that the stress of running a business is real, but notes that "stress can also be fuel if you harness it the right way. It forces you to evolve and make sharper decisions." To keep his stress productive, he is firm in setting boundaries and knowing when to switch off and make space for joy and rest, whether that means playing with the dogs, working in his garden, or escaping on a trip.

Palak Shah's business model is all about working with high-achieving women. Every day, she talks to women "who are outwardly successful but inwardly stretched thin. They have income but not stability. They're constantly earning, but rarely exhaling." Palak's goal is to give her clients structure, community, and the confidence to trust themselves. Her biggest advice for people in this situation: "Don't separate who you are from what you build. Let your family see your purpose. Let your business reflect your values. And never apologize—for going all in, or for stepping back. Both can be sacred."

Stepping back is a scary idea for many entrepreneurs. We're so used to constantly pushing forward that putting that progress on hold can feel like the ground just dropped out from under you. But sometimes that's exactly what needs to happen. A lot of us have been going full-throttle as both a business leader and a parent for years, with maybe an occasional vacation (that you probably still work during, if you're like many entrepreneurs). That sustained stress wears you down, sometimes to the point that the recovery strategies I've talked about just aren't going to cut it.

This is the exact reason why the sabbatical exists, although ironically, the people who likely need them the most—parents who own their own business—rarely think of them as an option. Sabbaticals are par for the course for religious leaders, which makes sense since the concept originates in the Bible. Every 7 years, the Israelites were told to take a year-long break from working the fields. That 7-year schedule is used by modern clergy, too, and in academia, where it's standard for professors to get them. Sabbaticals are also often offered to high-level executives in industries like technology and finance, roles where high stress and pressure make burnout a big risk.

You know who else deals with high stress and burnout risk? Entrepreneurs. We're living with constant financial pressure, high-stakes decision-making, and responsibility for other people's livelihoods. But unlike other industries, the typical entrepreneurial culture treats taking time off like it's the same as giving up, or a sign we're weak or uncommitted. Well, I'm here as your business mentor to tell you that's bullshit. Those industries offering sabbaticals understand something many entrepreneurs have forgotten. Sometimes, the most productive thing you can do is step back and remember who you are when you're not being productive at all. Sabbaticals aren't just about fixing what's broken or having time to rest. They're a chance to realign and answer bigger questions like "What do I want from the next phase of my life?" and "Is this what I actually want to be doing?"

I'm in the planning stages of a sabbatical of my own and, y'all, it's a bit scary. There's the fear of losing momentum or clients moving on, or even discovering that I actually hate my business. Beyond that, I honestly don't know what I want on the other side of my time away. I've been an entrepreneur for so long that I genuinely don't know who I am without my business identity, what my natural energy levels are, or what will come out once I create space for it. But I'm excited to learn these answers, and the only way I will is by putting the business on pause.

I've also noticed that I'm not the only one doing this. Over the past year, I've seen an emerging trend of female entrepreneurs stepping away from their businesses because they're exhausted and searching for something they can't name. They've achieved what everyone told them they should want: successful businesses, financial freedom, and thriving families. But somewhere along the way, they became executives optimizing their lives, rather than protagonists living them.

Something that doesn't get talked about enough is that you can have all the business systems in the world and still burn out from life. My business runs like a well-oiled machine, with processes and procedures and backup plans for my backup plans. But I never built those same systems for my personal life. It's hard to set boundaries on family drama or create sustainable rhythms for caregiving. One of the most profound realizations I've had in the past year was how little permission I've given myself to not be okay. I expected myself to handle every family crisis and unexpected challenge without missing a beat. I imagine I'm not the only entrepreneur who's treated their personal life like a startup; constantly in crisis mode and perpetually putting out fires. It's no wonder so many of us are exhausted.

If you're reading this and wondering whether you need your own sabbatical, that wondering itself might be your answer. This doesn't need to mean taking a whole year off. Maybe your sabbatical is permission to say no to everything that's non-essential for the next three months, or one afternoon a week with your phone turned off. The format isn't what matters. It's about giving yourself permission to be human in a culture that expects you to be superhuman, and building a life that includes success instead of being consumed by it.

Key Takeaways:

- **Self-care isn't selfish; it's strategic**: You can't make good business decisions when you're running on empty. Taking care of yourself is how you show up at your best for your business and family.

- **Watch for your warning signs**: Getting sick more often, checking email at 11 p.m., snapping at your kids, doing impossible math (trying to give 80% to three different things). These are signals you need to recalibrate.

- **Build resilience systems before you need them**: My 72-hour rule, Three-Person rule, and Minimum Viable Day aren't for when things are going well; they're for when multiple crises hit at once, and I can't think straight.

- **Permission to step back**: Sabbaticals aren't just for professors and clergy. Sometimes the most productive thing you can do is remember who you are when you're not being productive.

- **You're human, not a business problem**: Feeling tired or unmotivated doesn't mean you're broken. Maybe it's your internal wisdom telling you to slow down before you burn out completely.

CHAPTER 23

The Village You Need (And Why You Can't Do This Alone)

The saying "It takes a village to raise a child" also applies to businesses. No successful entrepreneur builds their company entirely on their own. Even solopreneurs need some kind of support system. Actually, folks who are a team of one might rely on their support system the most because the truth is, being an entrepreneur can be very lonely and isolating. That's a problem beyond just how it can impact your mental health (although that's important, too).

From a business standpoint, the biggest problem that comes from being isolated as a founder is that you can end up making ill-informed decisions. Without a community, you don't have anyone to brainstorm with or bounce ideas off of. This gets back to another common saying: you don't know what you don't know. Someone might have already found an easy solution to whatever issue you're facing, but that can't help you if you don't know about it. Other entrepreneurs are an invaluable knowledge resource who can share tools and strategies they've tried. If nothing else, they can at least relate to your frustrations, validate them, and help you talk through potential workarounds. All entrepreneurs, regardless of industry, understand each other on a certain level because they all face the same risks and pressures; things that people who don't own a business usually can't relate to.

It's very possible I'm preaching to the choir here. If you're a business owner, you probably are well aware of just how lonely that life can be. The question you're likely asking is: what's the best way to break the pattern of isolation? Some of the things I mentioned in earlier chapters can apply here. For instance, the three-person rule I have in my resilience systems from Chapter 22 is a form of leveraging my community. I didn't build those relationships just so that I would have someone to fall back on in a crisis, but having them there is absolutely a lifesaver when I'm struggling.

Finding a third life, as I talked about in Chapter 15, can be a big help here, too. The people in your third life probably won't be the ones who can help you answer questions about your cash flow or how to optimize your sales funnel, but they can keep you grounded in the real world when business stress is threatening to consume your life and send you into a spiral. That's one of the benefits of having a community: they're people who can broaden your viewpoint beyond your own perception and help you keep things in perspective.

Just like I have three different people I call in a crisis, it's smart to have different types of communities you can fall back on as a business owner. Building a diverse group of people around you means you have access to a broader mix of viewpoints. Basically, you're playing the odds. The more personalities and life experiences are in your network, the higher the chances one of them will have an answer for any given question. This can include people who have nothing to do with your business, like friends, family, fellow parents, or members of your church. All of these people together provide your emotional, personal support system, necessary for maintaining your mental health when your stress levels skyrocket or when you need advice on general life things.

The other entrepreneurs in your community are likely to have a more specific role than your more general support system. For instance, you might want to find an accountability partner who will hold you to your focus commitments, or a group of other professionals committed to deep work and execution. Or maybe you need a systems ally who excels at building and maintaining systems and can strengthen your operational foundation, or reality checkers who can help you maintain your perspective when Shiny Object Syndrome strikes. What you get from your community doesn't need to be set in stone. It's really about what kind of support you need. The most important thing is to find people who can relate to the unique challenges of owning a business, and who can offer support and advice that's based on lived experience, not generic cliches.

Other entrepreneurs in your industry are going to be able to offer the most specific, practical advice. These are the people who will understand your sales cycles and customers, and are most likely to be tuned into the latest industry news and trends. You can talk to them about specific sales tactics or marketing campaigns and what's worked for them (and what hasn't). They can also help you find the right suppliers or the best places to recruit new team members who have the exact skills that businesses in your niche need. Entrepreneurs from other industries can still be valuable connections, though they're more likely to be helpful with big-picture concepts like financial management, team building, or company culture; things that are often very similar across industries.

Part of the value of building a village is that you can learn from people who have more experience or different skills than you do. Robert Patin is another strong believer in the importance of a support system. He's very self-reliant in general, and probably could figure out solutions to his problems on his own, but sees his support network as an accelerator. As he says, "The quicker that I find a community or a person that has the experience I'm looking for, the faster that I can grow and improve."

But expertise isn't the only value of connecting with an entrepreneur group. I've been privileged to be in rooms, masterminds, and conversations with a lot of other business leaders over the years. A lot of them are people who look like they've got everything figured out from the outside. What I've learned from seeing their behind-the-scenes, though, is that even those high-profile entrepreneurs are still wrestling with the same decisions and making some things up as they go. A lot of the people who seem like they're so far ahead of you are secretly asking the same questions you are, things like "Do I even want this business anymore?" and "What am I supposed to do next?" Of course, they're not going to publicize that they feel this way. You only realize they're grappling with the same challenges when you spend time in spaces where they feel comfortable being honest and vulnerable. And, once you do, that can help you give yourself permission to not have all the answers. It takes a lot of confidence to let "I'm still figuring that out" function as a complete sentence, and engaging with other business leaders at your level (or above) is a very useful step in developing that confidence.

One key figure who is often a part of an entrepreneur's support system is a business coach or mentor. I started working with my first business coach about ten years ago, when I was growing E by Design, and the things I learned from her were a huge help in scaling that business to what would ultimately be a 7-figure exit. The key, of course, is to find the right mentor or coach for you and your business, and there's unfortunately no magic formula I can share to help you do that. You can reference back to that general advice on avoiding Guru Traps I gave in Chapter 8. Beyond that baseline, it comes down to whether your personalities and communication styles align. If you don't feel comfortable having an honest conversation with a coach, they're not the right coach for you, whatever accolades or success testimonials they can brag about.

Something else to remember is that what you need from a coach or mentor is going to change as your business grows and your life evolves. Even though I learned a lot from my first coach, I ended up changing to a different one after a few years. This is natural. The best coaches have a defined niche that you may no longer fit into down the line. If you start off working with a startup coach, for example, their advice will likely get less useful once you're ready to grow. At that point, you'll be better off working with someone who specializes in scaling businesses and can guide you through those unique challenges.

When it comes to connecting with other entrepreneurs, I've formed my network mostly through mastermind groups. When you join a mastermind group, you not only form relationships with the other members. Each of those people has their own networks they can introduce you to, which makes being in the group an entryway into a broader community. I met Brittany Pickrem through a mastermind, and her experience with it was similar to my own. At first, it terrified her to spend so much money on herself, because that's the main downside of these programs: the best ones often have pretty high price tags, and while they're absolutely worth it if you choose the right group, that's not always an easy investment to justify. But for Brittany (and me) joining that group put us in the same room as other high-achieving entrepreneurs, and that experience was transformative. As Brittany says, "I was absolutely the dumbest person in the room, and that was exactly where I needed to be." I also appreciate Brittany's perspective on making that kind of high-ticket investment: "Money is energy. When you put a lot of money into something, you're basically saying I bet that I'm going to make this worth it."

There are also ways to connect with other business leaders without needing to pay for the privilege. Every town has a chamber of commerce, and while some of these are more active than others, they often host networking get-togethers, workshops, and similar events where you can meet other local entrepreneurs. Many towns also have groups for women in business or other entrepreneurial meet-up organizations. These are groups you won't necessarily stumble on by accident, that can happen, but it's more likely you'll need to be proactive about searching them out. It's kind of like when you're a new parent. You do things like going to story hour at the library or mommy and me classes, and end up making friends with the other parents. Business meet-ups are the same concept, just swapping in your company for your kid as the reason you're all in the same place.

To connect with people outside your local area, joining professional organizations can be a big help. Just like local groups, these associations often host events like conferences, workshops, and seminars. This isn't a completely free option; most professional associations have a membership fee, and there's often an additional cost for events. Still, those fees are usually much lower than the cost to join a mastermind group, so they can be easier to fit into a tight budget.

You can also take advantage of social media. TikTok has a growing community of parent entrepreneurs, for instance. I also find Substack can be a valuable resource for this. There are tons of business-oriented communities that are very active and engaged. The people who join these groups are eager to read, learn, share knowledge, and make genuine connections, not just to consume whatever content gets served up to them by an algorithm.

Now, just like with coaches, not everybody you meet who owns a business is going to be a good source of advice. Jim Cocks made a good point when I talked to him about this. He's another big believer in community, saying, "I've always surrounded myself with successful mentors and entrepreneurs, and I believe in learning from others. But you've also got to make decisions that are right for *you*. Don't just chase shiny objects."

I know, I've said that before about other things, but it applies here, too. I've seen people bounce from one group to another without taking the time to actually build meaningful relationships. You might get a few drabbles and snippets of useful insight doing this, but you won't get the full value that a community can bring you. The better approach is to pick a few targeted groups to try out and commit to being active with those groups before you add any more.

You also want to pick the right events and people for your goals and where you are with your business. That means you need to figure that out before you start searching for events to attend or groups to join. Get specific about what you want to get out of it. Are you looking for deep industry insights? General advice on how to grow? Or maybe what you need right now is to be around people who will nod understanding when you talk about answering client emails in the school pickup line. Identify the main common denominator that would unite people in your ideal group, and use that to guide your decision of which ones to invest time in.

I'll give an example here. There used to be a massive convention every year called Funnel Hacking Live that drew people from a huge range of industries. If you wanted advice on how to optimize your sales funnel, you could go there to learn and meet lots of other people with the same goal. That said, if you just started your business and are still figuring out what a "sales funnel" even is, Funnel Hacking Live would be an overwhelming and expensive waste of time. The conference was designed for experienced sales professionals, and 97% of the material would be over a beginner's head.

The same idea applies to every type of entrepreneur support. With coaches or mastermind leaders, you want to find people who teach at your level. If you're brand new and find yourself in the same group as people doing $5 million in revenue, odds are you've been sold a bill of goods. This is a less expensive mistake when you're talking about a free group or professional organization, but you can still end up wasting your time or getting bad advice if you choose the wrong ones. Community is important for an entrepreneur, and you want to approach finding yours with the same intentional focus you'd bring to choosing a new supplier or hiring an employee. When you do that and put in the effort to build those connections, that's when you unlock their real value.

Key Takeaways:

- **Be strategic about which communities you join**: I chose a digital marketing group because that's exactly what RSG Sales needed. Match the community to your actual business stage and goals.

- **The real value is the people**: My biggest ROI from that mastermind wasn't the curriculum; it was the three key hires I made from connections in the group.

- **Build diverse support**: You need industry peers for tactical advice, other entrepreneurs for big-picture strategy, and friends/family to keep you sane.

- **Don't go it alone**: Your community is an accelerator. Stop wasting years figuring out what someone could teach you in months.

- **Depth over breadth:** Pick a few communities and actually build relationships instead of group-hopping.

CHAPTER 24

Your Business Is Grown—Now What?

Let's talk about transitions. They're scary. No way around that. Your business or your life shifts, and suddenly you're facing a future that looks nothing like what you planned.

But here's the thing about transitions: they're also exhilarating. There's something about standing at the edge of what's next that can make you feel alive. And if you're making the decision to sell your business, that's worth celebrating. Yes, celebrating. No matter why you're doing it. Burned out? Celebrate that you're choosing yourself. Ready for what's next? Celebrate that growth. Built something valuable? Celebrate that payday. This is a milestone, not a failure.

Building a business is a lot like raising a child in this way, too. You'll always be your kids' parents. But that shifts into a more passive, less hands-on role once they're adults. And that's a good thing. It's a sign you taught them the skills they need to stand on their own. (It's okay if you still see them in your mind as the 5-year-old holding your hand.)

Palak Shah said something that really stuck with me: "At some point, you'll hit a wall. Not because your business isn't working, but because it's working in a way that no longer works for you. That's your signal to evolve. The biggest threat to your growth isn't failure; it's success that traps you."

Deciding whether it's the right time to sell? It's one of the most difficult decisions that a founder needs to make. In my time talking to and working with other entrepreneurs, I've seen four main reasons that people want to sell. And here's what I want you to hear: all four of these reasons are valid. There's no "wrong" reason to exit your business.

One is the founder who's sick and tired of their business. They just don't want to lead it anymore. Sometimes you fall out of love with what you built. It happens. The passion fades. The work feels like drudgery instead of purpose. If that's you, you're not a failure—you're human. (P.S. This is where I was with E by Design.)

Another group is people whose business is struggling. They want to sell it to salvage something from all of their work. Not every business makes it. And that's not a reflection on you as a person or even as an entrepreneur. Selling before it completely tanks is smart. It's strategic. Don't let anyone make you feel like you're giving up.

Then there are the people who love their business but are burned out. Exhausted. They need a break. At the core, they still love what they do; they just can't do it right now. This one hits close to home for a lot of us. You've given everything you have, and you're running on fumes. That doesn't mean you failed. It means you're fucking human and you need rest.

And then there are those who love their business but are ready to do something that's better aligned to their current passions. This last group is usually comprised of serial entrepreneurs. They enjoy the startup and growth phases, but they get bored quickly once the business is established.

You can make it work in any of those situations. The specific steps you'll take in each case will vary. But there are also some universal steps that you can take once you're sure you want to sell your business, for any reason.

Here's the most important thing, and I can't stress this enough. Make sure that you actually want to sell. I've worked with companies in the past that thought they wanted out of the business, only to get cold feet once the process was in motion. (You may need to step back from the day-to-day, but more on that in a bit.)

Alright, so once you're committed to selling, here's what you need to do next. Get your financial house in order. This is the first thing that any buyer is going to look at when they're determining their offer. They'll want to see that your EBITDA (Earnings before interest, taxes, depreciation, and amortization) is strong; however, that's defined for your industry. They'll want to see that you've kept good records of your revenue and expenses so they can evaluate whether they stand to see a return on their investment if they buy it. (And if your books are a mess right now, don't panic. Just hire a good bookkeeper to clean them up. It's fixable.)

After that, you need to make sure the business is truly ready to function without you. And let me tell you, this is harder than it sounds for some businesses.

We get phone calls and emails all the time about selling RSG Sales. It's flattering, honestly. But here's the thing: the company's IP is tied up in my head and Josh's head. We don't have high-level account executives who could do what we do. Plus? We don't want to work for anyone else. So selling isn't an option for us right now. Sure, this could change if we brought in the talent. But for us, that would add a level of complexity to the business that we just don't want to mess with.

So once you've done all that legwork to make sure the business is ready to sell, here's where it gets interesting. How much do you want for it? The first thing you need to figure out is what assets within the business will actually be valuable for potential buyers.

This can be a very humbling experience. Because not everything you think is valuable will be an asset from a buyer's standpoint. And let me tell you, that can sting.

When I sold E by Design, we had 2-3 years of designs ready to go into production. I thought this would add to the value. I was proud of those designs. We'd put hours into them. Turns out, it didn't. Those designs were digital files that hadn't yet been tested in the market. If I'd held them back, it wouldn't have affected the valuation at all. I remember feeling so aggravated by that. Like, "Wait, all that work doesn't count?" But that's the reality.

What ended up being E by Design's valuable assets were our accounts, current designs, and business systems. The things that a buyer could immediately put to use, earning verified revenue after the sale.

Same thing with Danielle Ratliff's experience selling her massage business. On the surface, you might think things like her team of massage therapists or the building she worked out of would be assets. But the building was leased, which made it a liability, not an asset. And employees can come and go, so they're not worth much when it comes to a sale.

What she was really selling was her reputation and client list. Things that would give the new owner a book of business to start from. When a buyer can see a guarantee of future revenue, that's what makes them want to buy the business.

Figuring out which business assets are valuable and how much you can ask for them isn't always easy, especially for a founder who hasn't bought or sold a business before. It's more straightforward in businesses that have a lot of physical assets. Like a manufacturing company that owns its own production equipment. Or a product seller with significant inventory.

Even in these cases, though, there will be intangibles that factor into that value. Things like your brand recognition or intellectual property, like patents or proprietary recipes and formulas. Established client contracts. Your repeat customer base. For example, the owner of an independent bookstore in my area recently sold it for $250,000. Part of that value was the physical book inventory. But they also had the support of local book clubs, who had been buying their books at the store for years. Those guaranteed ongoing sales were a significant value add on top of the inventory and systems.

Here's where I'm going to give you some advice that saved me a ton of headaches. Work with a business broker or evaluation company. They'll make sure you're correctly identifying the most salable parts of your company. And asking for the full value for them. These professionals are experts in selling businesses. They know exactly what buyers look for. I worked with a broker when I sold E by Design, and that was a huge help in figuring out the company's true assets. What asking price would be reasonable? (They were worth every penny I paid them, honestly.)

Alright, that's the selling route. But maybe you don't want to sell. Maybe you just need to step back from the day-to-day grind. If that's you, here's what you need to know - you start the same way as selling. Make sure the business has the right systems to run without you. Get your financial house in order.

Now you need to figure out what YOU want? How do you want to be part of the business you built?

Here's where we need to go back to the basics. What is your Zone of Genius? Where do you bring the most value to the company? What parts light you up? When you can answer those questions, you can hire or offload everything else to someone else. It really is that simple.

Let me give you a little pro tip I learned. I also put a time limit on how much I wanted to work in an average week. For me, it is two to three hours per week. This way, I can focus on the marketing that brings in the leads and the financial side of things, so I can make sure the business stays healthy.

Look, I'm not naive. I know stepping way back can feel like you are cutting off a hand. But you need to trust the business and team you have built. If you nitpick and try to control the very things you wanted to give up, then you are just sabotaging yourself, the business, and your team.

I know that I can sound like a broken record at times, but I feel the need to say this statement again. YOU ARE NOT YOUR BUSINESS. IT IS ITS OWN LIVING AND BREATHING ENTITY!

Being too attached to your business is exactly what happened to Danielle Ratliff. Looking back, she says, "If I could do it over, I would have exited sooner." If she had, she wouldn't have driven herself to the extreme level of burnout she ended up experiencing. And she thinks she would've made more off the sale, too.

Her advice for other business owners? "It's not worth your health or your sanity. Sometimes you do need to blow it up and make the hard decisions."

Listen to that. Really listen. Because I see so many entrepreneurs (myself included sometimes) holding on way too long. Thinking if we just push a little harder, work a little more, sacrifice a little more, it'll all work out. But at what cost?

And look, you don't need to follow anyone else's pattern or timeline when it comes to stepping back from your business. The goal is to find an arrangement that supports the life you want now. And for the foreseeable future. That could mean hiring a COO and shifting into a visionary role, but that's not your only option. There's no one "right" way to do this. (Despite what all the business gurus on LinkedIn will tell you.)

Take Nick Rodsater's wife, Stef, for example. She took the lead on marketing when they first started the business. But she's recently decided to go down to part-time hours. This decision, Nick says, "has had so many benefits for our family. She gets to homeschool our kids and spend almost every morning with them and truly raise and develop them." While some of their marketing campaigns have lost energy without Stef there to drive them, that trade-off was worth it for their family.

And then there are people like Brittany Pickrem who don't want to sell or step back at all.

Brittany Pickrem is one of those entrepreneurs who truly loves what she does. She doesn't ever really want to walk away from her design business. In her vision of the future, she says, "I hope one day that my retirement is that I'm working with fewer clients and bigger budgets. I never really want to let that go." Currently, she's building her eco-friendly detergent business. Her plan is for that revenue stream to give her the freedom to be more selective about the clients she works with. To niche down on just the specific types of work that truly energize her. That's her version of success, and it doesn't look like anyone else's.

Nobody can tell you when it's time to make a change. Not me, not your mentor, not your spouse. But here's the thing: you'll know because you'll stop being able to ignore it. It shows up in your Sunday night anxiety. In how you talk about the business at dinner parties. In how you feel on Monday mornings. The decision keeps tapping you on the shoulder until you turn around and deal with it.

Whether that change means selling, closing, or just stepping way back? That part depends on what you actually want. If the business still excites you, but it's eating your life, step back and hire people to run the day-to-day. If you're *done*-done, if there's no part of it you want to touch anymore, then sell or close it. But both require the same first step: admitting that what you're doing right now isn't working.

So if you already know something needs to change, and you've known for a while, what are you waiting for?

Key Takeaways:

- **Work through your emotions before you start looking for buyers**: Changing your mind midway creates chaos.

- **Get your systems and finances in order**: Buyers want to see immediate revenue potential.

- **Not everything you've built is valuable to a buyer**: Hire a business broker to help with due diligence.

- If you want to keep the business but get your life back, hire someone to run operations and define clear boundaries.

- **Exit while the business is thriving**: A burned-out founder kills value fast.

The Life Cycle of a Business

Building a business is like raising a kid. Both go through seasons.

Spring is planting seeds and rebirth. Newborn chaos and startup chaos. Every sale is a win, every setback feels massive because you've never dealt with it before.

Summer is growth; long days, lots of action. School drop-offs and dance recitals for kids. Team building and revenue milestones for your business.

Fall is harvest. Your kids get independent. Your business is established with consistent revenue. You can finally think big picture instead of just surviving.

Winter is rest. Empty nest. For your business, it's when you sell, pull back, or hold steady while you figure out what's next.

I have loved each and every season with my kids. If I'm being 100% honest, I've not always had the same feelings about my businesses, but I believe that is a normal part of growing as a human and entrepreneur.

I'm in winter right now. Kids are grown, RSG runs itself, and I'm only making decisions that are right for me. This is the first time I've ever stopped and really thought about what I actually want next.

I didn't decide to become an entrepreneur. I stumbled into it, building businesses based on other people's skills or ideas. This newsletter and this book? First things I've done just for me. Took me way too long. I was so busy worrying about everybody else that I lost touch with what I wanted.

Here's what I've learned: there is no perfect time. There will always be someone who needs you, another revenue opportunity, another family crisis, another reason to wait. The universe isn't going to hand you permission. You have to take it.

What that looks like is different for everyone. Palak Shah weaves her children into her business world. As she says, "The greatest gift I've decided to give my children is a mother who is fully herself, and fully happy. For parents who are struggling: your life is not an inconvenience to your success. Build a business that reflects your values. Build integration, build support, and most of all, build with honesty."

As a parent or business owner, definitely when you're both, there will always be chaos. Competing priorities. Days when your to-do list grows faster than you can work through it. If you wait for the perfect time, you'll wait forever.

You know that thing you've been putting off? Start it now. It won't go perfectly, but it wouldn't anyway. Nothing does. Stop ranking your dreams as less important than everyone else's needs.

Guess what? What you wanted ten years ago isn't what you want today. That's normal. Maybe your business was your dream when you started, but now you're ready for something new. Pia Silva told me something that stuck: if you're embarrassed by what you did a few years ago, it means you're growing. For her, "that gave me the perspective I needed to be seen and go out there imperfectly, which is one of the most important things you can do for a business."

That's not just important for business, it's how you should live.

Go after what's in your heart, however messy it gets. Stop living by someone else's timeline. It's your business, your family, your life. You know what you want. So what are you waiting for?

A Note Before You Go

Hey friend!

If you've made it to this page, I want you to hear something clearly: I'm beyond thrilled that you're here.

Writing this book wasn't just about sharing strategies or stories; it was about telling the truth. The real truth. The kind that only comes from raising a business and a family and somehow remembering who you are in the middle of all of it.

If something in these pages made you feel seen or less alone or a little more hopeful about your next season, then I've done my job.

But I don't want this to be the end of our conversation.

Every week, I write *Now What, Y'all?* A newsletter for women like us who are building, evolving, questioning, dreaming, and trying to create a life that actually feels like ours.

It's where I share what's really happening behind the scenes: the honest parts, the messy parts, the lessons I'm learning in real time, and the tiny shifts that make a big difference.

And it's where a growing community of entrepreneurs and parents remind each other that we don't have to figure all of this out alone.

If that sounds like a place you'd like to be, I'd love to welcome you.

Come join us: *www.nowwhatyall.com*

Ready? Let's do this together.

xx, Heather